ARL Annual Salary Survey 2011–2012

Compiled and Edited by

Martha Kyrillidou

Shaneka Morris

Association of Research Libraries

Washington, DC

2012

ARL Annual Salary Survey 2011–2012

The quantitative tables presented in this publication are not indicative of performance and should not be used as measures of library quality. In comparing any individual library to ARL medians or to other ARL members, one must be careful to make such comparisons within the context of differing institutional characteristics.

Custom reports based on the *Salary Survey* data are also available. Contact the ARL Statistics and Measurement Program Officer for further information.

Visit the ARL Statistics and Assessment Program online at http://www.arl.org/stats/.

Published by the
Association of Research Libraries
Washington, DC 20036
www.arl.org

ISSN 0361-5669
ISBN 1-59407-875-0 / 978-1-59407-875-0 print
ISBN 1-59407-893-9 / 978-1-59407-893-4 online

The paper used in this publication meets the minimum requirements of the American National Standard for Information Science and National Information Standards Organization standard—Permanence of Paper for Publications and Documents in Libraries and Archives, ANSI/NISO Z39.48-1992(R1997).

CONTENTS

ARL University Law Libraries

Salary Survey Trends 2011–2012

The *ARL Annual Salary Survey 2011–2012* reports salary data for all professional staff working in Association of Research Libraries (ARL) member libraries. ARL represents the interests of libraries that serve major North American research institutions. The Association operates as a forum for the exchange of ideas and as an agent for collective action to influence forces affecting the ability of these libraries to meet the future needs of scholarship. The ARL Statistics and Assessment program, which produces the *Salary Survey*, is organized around collecting, analyzing, and distributing quantifiable information describing the characteristics of research libraries. The *ARL Annual Salary Survey* is the most comprehensive and thorough guide to current salaries in large US and Canadian academic and research libraries and is a valuable management and research tool.

Data for 9,910 professional staff members were reported this year for the 115 ARL university libraries, including their law and medical libraries (930 staff members reported by 72 medical libraries and 742 staff members reported by 77 law libraries). For the 11 nonuniversity ARL members, data were reported for 4,046 professional staff members.

The tables are organized in seven major sections. The first section includes Tables 1 through 4, which report salary figures for all professionals working in ARL member libraries, including law and medical library data. The second section includes salary information for the 11 nonuniversity research libraries of ARL. The third section, entitled "ARL University Libraries," reports data in Tables 7 through 25 for the "general" library system of the university ARL members, combining US and Canadian data but excluding law and medical data. The fourth section, composed of Tables 26 through 30, reports data on US ARL university library members excluding law and medical data. The fifth section (Tables 31–34) reports data on Canadian ARL university libraries excluding law and medical data. The sixth section (Tables 35–41) and the seventh section (Tables 42–48) report on medical and law libraries, respectively, combining US and Canadian data.

The university population is generally treated in three distinct groups: staff in the "general" library system, staff in the university medical libraries, and staff in the university law libraries. Any branch libraries for which data were received, other than law and medical, are included in the "general" category, whether or not those libraries are administratively independent. Footnotes for many institutions provide information on branch inclusion or exclusion.

In all tables where data from US and Canadian institutions are combined, Canadian salaries are converted into US dollar equivalents at the rate of 1.0014 Canadian dollars per US dollar.[1] Tables 4 and 31 through 34, however, pertain exclusively to staff in Canadian university libraries, so salary data in those tables are expressed in Canadian dollars.

---

1 This is the average monthly noon exchange rate published in the *Bank of Canada Review* for the period July 2010–June 2011 and is used in converting figures that are shown effective as of 1 July 2011. This information can be accessed at: http://www.bankofcanada.ca/en/rates/exchange.html.

Race and Ethnicity

There were 1,233 minority professional staff reported in 99 US ARL university libraries, including law and medical libraries.[2] Note that the data for minority professionals comes only from the US ARL university libraries following the Equal Employment Opportunity Commission (EEOC) definitions; Canadian law prohibits the identification of Canadians by ethnic category.

Currently, 14.2% of the professional staff in US ARL university libraries (including law and medical libraries) belong to one of the four non-Caucasian categories for which ARL keeps records. The percentage of minorities in managerial or leadership positions in the largest US academic libraries is far lower: 7.1% are directors (8 out of 112), 6.7% are associate directors (22 out of 326), 8.8% are assistant directors (14 out of 160), and 9.2% (40 out of 433) are the head of a branch library (see Table 27). Figure 1, below, depicts the overall racial/ethnic distribution of professional staff in US ARL university libraries: Caucasian/Other 85.8%, Asian/Pacific Islander 6.8%, Black 4.4%, Hispanic 2.6%, and American Indian/Alaskan Native 0.3%.

Figure 1: Ethnicity/Race of Professional Staff in US ARL University Libraries, FY 2011–2012

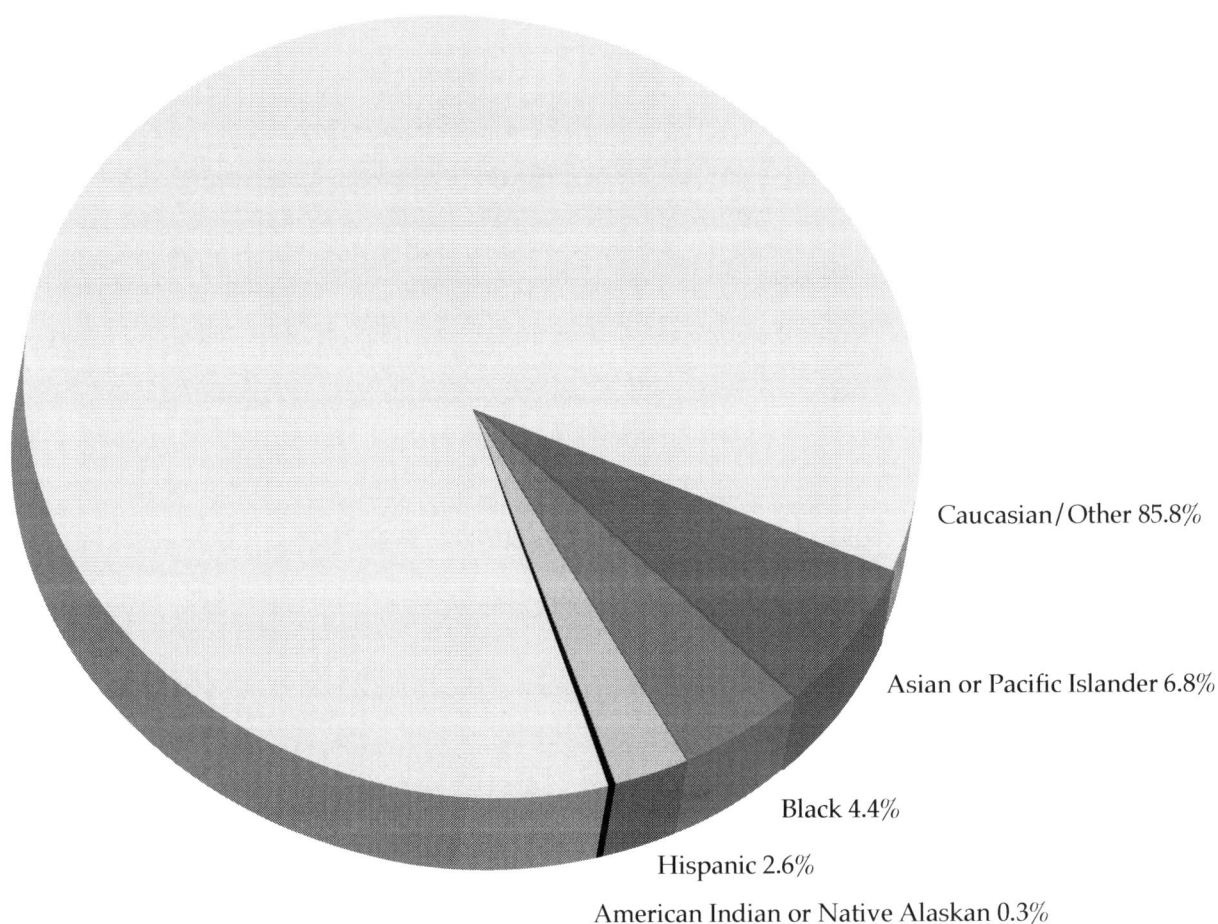

Caucasian/Other 85.8%

Asian or Pacific Islander 6.8%

Black 4.4%

Hispanic 2.6%

American Indian or Native Alaskan 0.3%

---

2 Some US institutions offer their librarians the option of not reporting race and ethnicity; others forbid the tracking of racial and ethnic classification altogether. See Footnotes.

Minority professional staff in US ARL university libraries continues to be disproportionately distributed across the country. Using Figure 2, we can compare the number of minority staff with other staff, region by region. These patterns of distribution have been relatively stable for the entire history of ARL's data-collection experience. Minorities are underrepresented by over 30% in the West North Central region and by more than 28% in the New England region (see Table 25 for a definition of the regions). Proportionately to other regions, there are more minorities in the Pacific, South Atlantic, West South Central, and Middle Atlantic regions.

Figure 2: Minority Professionals by Region in US ARL University Libraries, FY 2011–2012

	New England	Middle Atlantic	East North Central	West North Central	South Atlantic	East South Central	West South Central	Mountain	Pacific	TOTAL	%
Race/Ethnicity Category											
Black	35	67	70	23	107	22	27	7	29	387	31%
Hispanic	19	40	26	10	31	7	33	19	42	227	18%
Asian	76	96	74	23	85	12	40	19	165	590	48%
AI/AN*	5	3	4	4	2	1	2	7	1	29	2%
Minority Total	135	206	174	60	225	42	102	52	237	1,233	100%
Minority Percent	10.90%	16.70%	14.10%	4.90%	18.20%	3.40%	8.30%	4.20%	19.20%		
Nonminority Total	1,148	1,239	1,254	527	1,227	337	578	420	747	7,477	100%
Nonminority Percent	15.40%	16.60%	16.80%	7.00%	16.40%	4.50%	7.70%	5.60%	10.00%		
Regional Percent Total staff	14.70%	16.60%	16.40%	6.70%	16.70%	4.40%	7.80%	5.40%	11.30%		
Proportional Minority Representation	-28.69%	0.82%	-15.86%	-30.96%	11.20%	-24.42%	7.01%	-24.92%	92.39%		

* American Indian/Alaskan Native

According to Figure 3 below, women comprise 68.6% of racial/ethnic minority professional staff in US ARL university libraries, whereas 61.7% of non-minority professional staff are women. The overall gender balance in the 115 Canadian and US university libraries (including law and medical libraries) is 36.4% male and 63.6% female. See Figure 2, above, and Figure 3, below, for more detail on race/ethnic and gender distribution.

Figure 3: Race/Ethnicity and Sex Distribution of Professional Staff in ARL University Libraries, FY 2011–2012

UNITED STATES					
	Men		**Women**		**Total**
	Number of Staff	**Percent of Total**	**Number of Staff**	**Percent of Total**	
Main	2,788	38.4%	4,472	61.6%	7,260
Medical	245	29.8%	576	70.2%	821
Law	247	35.2%	454	64.8%	701
Minority*	387	31.4%	846	68.6%	1,233
Non-minority	2,861	38.3%	4,616	61.7%	7,477
All	3,248	37.3%	5,462	62.7%	8,710
CANADA					
	Men		**Women**		**Total**
	Number of Staff	**Percent of Total**	**Number of Staff**	**Percent of Total**	
Main	308	31.5%	670	68.5%	978
Medical	10	9.2%	99	90.8%	109
Law	13	31.7%	28	68.3%	41
All	331	29.3%	797	70.7%	1,128
UNITED STATES AND CANADA (COMBINED)					
	Men		**Women**		**Total**
	Number of Staff	**Percent of Total**	**Number of Staff**	**Percent of Total**	
Main	3,096	37.6%	5,142	62.4%	8,238
Medical	255	27.4%	675	72.6%	930
Law	260	35.0%	482	65.0%	742
All	3,611	36.4%	6,299	63.6%	9,910

* Includes staff in medical and law libraries.

Note: There are three US institutions that did not report race/ethnicity data; therefore, the totals will not aggregate to the total needed for the US and Canadian sub-totals to equal the figure displayed in the combined total.

ARL recognizes the difficulties that the profession has in attracting a diverse workforce and continues to work actively in the development of workplace climates that embrace diversity. The ARL Diversity Programs, through its Leadership and Career Development Program and the Initiative to Recruit a Diverse Workforce, emphasize ARL's and its members' commitment to creating a diverse academic and research library community to better meet the new challenges of global competition and changing demographics. Further, the Diversity Programs focus on issues surrounding work relationships in libraries while considering the impact of diversity on library services, interactions with library users, and the development of collections. More information about the Diversity Programs can be found at http://www.arl.org/diversity/.

ClimateQUAL® is an assessment initiative that focuses on some of the same issues. It is the Statistics and Assessment program's tool that assesses organizational climate and diversity in libraries. ClimateQUAL® helps libraries plumb the dimensions of climate and organizational culture important for a healthy organization in a library setting. The ClimateQUAL® survey addresses climate issues such as diversity, teamwork, learning, and fairness, as well as current managerial practices, and staff attitudes and beliefs. Libraries use their ClimateQUAL® data to improve their organizational climate and diversity culture for delivering superior services to the communities they serve. More information about ClimateQUAL® can be found at http://www.climatequal.org.

GENDER DATA

Many readers of previous surveys have inquired about evidence of gender-based salary differentials in ARL libraries. Additionally, data on salary comparisons for directors also are frequently requested. Since 2008–2009, the average salary for female directors was slightly higher than that of their male counterparts. However, for the second consecutive year the trend was reversed, with male directors earning more than female directors (see Table 17); furthermore, the number of women in the top administrative library position decreased to 65 out of 112 total director positions reported in 2011–2012 (see Table 17).

In keeping with previous years, the 2011–2012 data show that salaries for women in US ARL university libraries have not yet met parity with that of men (see Table 17). In 2011–2012 the overall salary for women was only 96.22% of that of men for the 115 ARL university libraries (compared to 96.05% in 2010–2011). This suggests a slow, long-term trend towards closure of the gender gap in ARL libraries — in 1980–1981, women in ARL libraries made roughly 87% that of men.

Table 17 displays 27 job categories; females earn more than their male counterparts in just 14 of the 27 categories listed. Table 18 provides average years of professional experience for many of the same staffing categories for which salary data are shown in Table 17, revealing that experience differentials may explain some differences within specific job categories. Women have more experience in all but two of the six job categories in which they average higher pay. However, there are four other categories in which women, on average, have more experience and less pay: Associate Director, Assistant Director, Functional Specialist, and Department Head-Other. Table 19 further reveals that the average salary for men is consistently higher than the average salary for women in all ten experience cohorts. Among minority librarians, the average salary for minority men is higher than that for minority women in nine of the ten experience cohorts (see Table 30).

There is a sense that the gender gap persists in academe in areas beyond the library and that a renewed commitment to resolve the problem is needed.[3] A variety of reasons have been offered as to why these trends persist, most notably the perception that work is peripheral in a woman's life and, consequently, female-dominated professions are undervalued. Librarianship is predominantly and persistently a woman's profession.

3 There are many instances citing the continuation of gender inequity in academia. See, for example: Mary Ann Mason, "Still Earning Less," *Chronicle of Higher Education* 13 January 2010 http://chronicle.com/article/Still-Earning-Less/63482/; Katherine Mangan, "Women in Academic Medicine: Equal to Men, Except in Pay," *Chronicle of Higher Education* 31 March 2010 http://chronicle.com/article/Women-in-Academic-Medicine-/64892/; Paula Wasley, "Gender Gap in Pay Widens Over Time," *Chronicle of Higher Education* 4 May 2007 http://chronicle.com/article/Gender-Gap-in-Pay-Widens-Over/9208/; Denise K. Manger's articles in the *Chronicle of Higher Education*, "Faculty Salaries Increased 3.7% in 1999–2000" (14 April 2000: A20) and "Faculty Salaries are Up 3.6%, Double the Rate of Inflation" (23 April 1999: A16); D. W. Miller, "Salary Gap Between Male and Female Professors Grows Over the Years, Study Suggests," *Chronicle of Higher Education*, Today's News, 27 April 2000; and Yolanda Moses, "Salaries in Academe: The Gender Gap Persists," *Chronicle of Higher Education* 12 December 1997: A60.

The scarcity of men in the profession has been well documented in many studies—the largest percentage of men employed in ARL libraries was 38.2% in 1980–1981; since then men have consistently represented about 35% of the professional staff in ARL libraries.

THE FUNCTIONAL SPECIALIST BREAKDOWN

In 2004, the ARL Statistics and Measurement Committee accepted a proposal from the ACRL Personnel Administrators and Staff Development Officers Discussion Group to break down the Functional Specialist category (FSPEC). The group's major concern was that so many different types of positions, with their varying job descriptions and salaries, were being labeled with the code FSPEC that data reported for the category were beginning to lose meaning. For each position that would have been labeled FSPEC in past years, the proposal offered ARL institutions two options: either use one of eight new codes to describe that position; or, if none of the eight new codes could adequately describe that position, use FSPEC. As seen in Figure 4, 17.2% of Functional Specialists in all libraries did not use an alternative code, a decrease over the 2010–2011 figures. As in 2010–2011, Archivists and Information Technology specialists comprised the largest percentage of Functional Specialists who used an alternative code (62.0%).

Figure 4: Distribution of Functional Specialist Job Sub-Codes by Type of Library

Position	Main		Medical		Law		All	
	No.	Percent	No.	Percent	No.	Percent	No.	Percent
Archivists	489	22.8%	17	10.8%	5	9.3%	511	21.7%
Business Manager	146	6.8%	11	7.0%	2	3.7%	159	6.8%
Human Resources	76	3.5%	0	0.0%	0	0.0%	76	3.2%
IT, Systems	396	18.5%	37	23.6%	14	25.9%	447	19.0%
IT, Web Developer	159	7.4%	21	13.4%	11	20.4%	191	8.1%
IT, Programmer	284	13.3%	26	16.6%	0	0.0%	310	13.2%
Media Specialist	119	5.6%	4	2.5%	4	7.4%	124	5.3%
Preservation	125	5.8%	2	1.3%	1	1.9%	128	5.4%
Other Functional Specialists	348	16.2%	39	24.8%	17	31.5%	404	17.2%
Total	**2,142**		**157**		**54**		**2,353**	

Figure 5, below, displays the average salaries of the subcategories by position and sex (law and medical libraries not included) in the same fashion as Table 17. The salaries in each of the sub-categories deviate widely from the combined Functional Specialist average salary of $66,472. Human resource specialists have the highest average of all subcategories, with an average salary of $73,334; media/multimedia specialists have the lowest average salary of $58,759.

Figure 5: Distribution of Functional Specialist Job Sub-Codes' Average Salaries by Sex[4]

Position	Women		Men		Total	
	Salary	**No.**	**Salary**	**No.**	**Salary**	**No.**
Archivists	60,157	319	65.083	170	61,869	489
Business Manager	73,141	91	71,995	55	72,709	146
Human Resources	72,837	63	75,746	13	73,334	76
IT, Systems	70,721	127	68,759	269	69,388	396
IT, Web Developer	64,102	69	65,744	90	65,032	159
IT, Programmer	71,006	71	71,675	213	71,508	284
Media Specialist	58,169	57	59,300	62	58,759	119
Preservation	65,051	87	69,502	38	66,404	125
Other Functional Specialists	64,782	224	69,255	124	66,376	348
All Functional Specialists	**65,313**	**1,108**	**68,273**	**1,034**	**66,742**	**2,142**

In regards to the gender gap in ARL libraries discussed in the previous section, it is worth noting that the average salaries of men are higher than those of women in seven out of the nine categories in Figure 5.

Institutional Characteristics and Salaries

A. Public and Private Institutions

The gap between salaries paid in private US ARL university libraries and those paid in publicly supported US university libraries increased in 2011–2012 to 8.5%, with librarians at private institutions earning an average of $5,939 more than their peers at public institutions. Out of 27 job categories, only in three (Head of Serials, Head of Rare Books/Manuscripts, and Head of Computer Systems) did librarians in public institutions earn more than their peers employed in private institutions (see Table 21).

B. Library Size

Library size, as measured by the number of professional staff, is another significant determinant of salary. As a rule, the largest libraries tend to pay the highest average salaries, not only overall, but for specific positions, as well. 2011–2012 data reflect this trend. The largest libraries, those with more than 110 staff, reported the highest average salary, $75,974, followed by libraries with between 75 and 110 staff, which reported an average salary of $75,910. The next highest average salary, $73,167, was reported by libraries with between 50 to 74 staff, followed by the smallest libraries, i.e., those with 13 to 49 staff, which reported an average salary of $72,562 (see Table 23). The gap between the highest paying cohort and the lowest paying cohort decreased in 2011–2012 to $3,412. The cutoff staffing levels used to determine the largest cohort of libraries, after declining in every year since 1995–1996,

---

4 The average salaries for All Functional Specialists published in the *ARL Annual Salary Survey 2009–2010* and *2010–2011* were not correct. The correct average salaries for 2010–2011 are $63,847 for women, $65,981 for men, and $64,852 overall. The correct average salaries for 2009–1010 are $62,070 for women, $64,299 for men, and $63,130 overall.

continued to hold steady at 110 in 2011–2012.[5]

C. GEOGRAPHIC AREA

In 2011–2012, the highest average salaries were found in Canada ($89,758) followed by New England ($79,946) with salaries in the Pacific region ($76,666) coming in third (see Table 25). The Canadian average salary has not been this high since 2008–2009 when it was $82,295. This sharp increase in Canadian salaries is due to fluctuations in the currency exchange rate. For the 2011–2012 survey period the Canadian currency exchange rate is 1.0014. The West South Central region had the lowest average salary: $64,036.

D. RANK STRUCTURE

Rank structure provides a useful framework for examining professional salaries in ARL university libraries. Figure 6, below, displays average salary and years of experience in the most commonly used rank structures. Readers should be aware that not all individuals have a rank that fits into the rank structure the library utilizes. Most commonly, directors may have no rank (or a rank outside the structure) and it is common for non-librarians included in the survey (business officers, personnel staff, computer specialists, liaisons, etc.) to be unranked, as well.

The pattern of relationships between rank and salary seen in past years continues: with higher rank associated with higher average years of experience and a correspondingly higher salary. 5,769 of the 8,238 librarians in ARL university member libraries occupy a rank within these three most commonly found ranking systems, and the largest number of professionals (3,443) occupy a position in a four-step rank structure.

Figure 6: Average Salaries and Average Years of Experience of Library Professionals in Libraries with Three, Four, and Five Step Rank Structures, FY 2011–2012

	Three-Step		Four-Step		Five-Step	
	Salary	**Experience**	**Salary**	**Experience**	**Salary**	**Experience**
Librarian 1	62,860	9.8	54,590	7.8	55,484	9.9
Librarian 2	72,918	18.1	60,845	12.4	65,899	13.9
Librarian 3	88,794	25.4	74,625	20.2	72,431	17.8
Librarian 4			91,125	26.7	87,073	23.6
Librarian 5					104,406	29.6
No. of Staff	**1,360**		**3,443**		**966**	

INFLATION EFFECT

Tables 2 and 6 reveal changes in beginning professional and median salaries as reported by both university and nonuniversity research libraries as well as the US Bureau of Labor's Cost of Living Index (CPI-All Urban Consumers). Table 3 is similar to Table 2, but reports data only on US libraries. Table 4 shows trend data for Canadian libraries and compares them to the changes in the Canadian Consumer Price Index (Consumer

---

[5] In 1995–1996, the largest cohort of libraries was determined based on staff over 124; in 1996–1998, over 120; in 1998-1999, over 115; and since 1999–2000, over 110. See Table 23.

Price Index for Canada, all-items, not seasonally adjusted). Tables 2, 3, and 4 include law and medical library staff in ARL university libraries. In contrast to 2010–2011, these tables indicate that the purchasing power of professionals in the United States did not keep pace with inflation, while the purchasing power of their Canadian counterparts did keep pace with inflation.

The median salary for US ARL university libraries in 2011 increased to $66,467 (see Table 3). This modest salary increase did not keep pace with the rebounding economy, which saw the US CPI increase by 3.6% (see Table 3).[6] In contrast, Canadian salaries (reported in Canadian dollars) surpassed inflation by 1.3 percentage points: the Canadian CPI increased 2.7%, while median salaries in Canadian university libraries increased by 4.0% to $85,551(Canadian dollars, see Table 4).[7] The difference in the exchange rates between 2010–2011 (1.0556 Canadian per U.S. dollar) and 2011–2012 (1.0014 Canadian per US dollar) contributed to these changes.

The median beginning salary (BPS) for university ARL librarians increased to $46,000 in 2011–2012 (see Table 2). Table 6 shows that nonuniversity librarians also experienced increases in their median and beginning salaries in 2011–2012, which increased to $95,046 and $51,630, respectively.

Readers are reminded that these data reflect only salaries, and that there are other compensation issues which may have influenced the pattern of salaries in various institutions. In addition, a highly standardized structure for capturing data has been used, which may portray results in a way that cannot be fully representative of a local situation.

Martha Kyrillidou
Shaneka Morris
Association of Research Libraries

---

6 CPI data retrieved from the US Department of Labor, Bureau of Labor Statistics' *Consumer Price Index-All Urban Consumers (US All items, 1982-84=100 - CUUR0000SA0)* available online at http://www.bls.gov/data/.

7 The source for Canadian CPI data is *Table 5: The Consumer Price Index for Canada (All-Items, Not Seasonally Adjusted, Historical Data)* published in *The Daily*, a Statistics Canada publication, available online at http://www.statcan.gc.ca/pub/62-001-x/2009010/t040-eng.htm.

SALARY LEVELS FOR STAFF IN ARL LIBRARIES

TABLES 1–4

TABLE 1: DISTRIBUTION BY SALARY LEVEL

Figures in columns headed by fiscal year show the number of filled professional positions. Columns headed by Cum. % show the percentage of all filled positions with salaries equal to or more than the beginning of each salary range.

Note: Canadian salaries are expressed in US dollars. Data includes medical and law libraries. The 78,000–78,999 salary range and the 79,000–79,999 salary range from the 2010–2011 publication have been collapsed to form the 78,000–79,999 salary range shown in the "FY 2010–2011" columns below.

Salary Range	University Libraries				Nonuniversity Libraries			
	FY 2010-2011	Cum. %	FY 2011-2012	Cum. %	FY 2010-2011	Cum. %	FY 2011-2012	Cum. %
More than 300,000	6	0.1%	8	0.1%	0	0.0%	0	0.0%
250,000 - 299,999	11	0.2%	13	0.2%	0	0.0%	0	0.0%
200,000 - 250,000	42	0.6%	51	0.7%	3	0.1%	4	0.1%
175,000 - 199,999	56	1.1%	60	1.3%	7	0.3%	8	0.3%
150,000 - 174,999	87	2.0%	107	2.4%	315	8.8%	317	8.1%
140,000 - 149,999	70	2.7%	68	3.1%	116	11.9%	138	11.5%
130,000 - 139,999	99	3.7%	134	4.5%	218	17.8%	233	17.3%
120,000 - 129,999	141	5.1%	173	6.2%	252	24.6%	258	23.7%
110,000 - 119,999	253	7.6%	322	9.4%	331	33.5%	389	33.3%
100,000 - 109,999	402	11.6%	395	13.4%	422	44.9%	464	44.8%
95,000 - 99,999	304	14.7%	309	16.5%	205	50.4%	249	50.9%
90,000 - 94,999	312	17.8%	350	20.1%	210	56.1%	227	56.5%
85,000 - 89,999	452	22.3%	489	25.0%	206	61.6%	241	62.5%
80,000 - 84,999	575	28.0%	589	31.0%	241	68.1%	296	69.8%
78,000 - 79,999	240	30.4%	247	33.5%	68	69.9%	117	72.7%
76,000 - 77,999	258	33.0%	274	36.2%	66	71.7%	85	74.8%
74,000 - 75,999	320	36.1%	315	39.4%	115	74.8%	111	77.5%
72,000 - 73,999	338	39.5%	358	43.0%	56	76.3%	61	79.0%
70,000 - 71,999	351	43.0%	351	46.5%	83	78.6%	59	80.5%
68,000 - 69,999	387	46.9%	405	50.6%	94	81.1%	117	83.4%
66,000 - 67,999	374	50.6%	370	54.4%	79	83.2%	98	85.8%
64,000 - 65,999	480	55.4%	400	58.4%	49	84.6%	60	87.3%
62,000 - 63,999	377	59.1%	411	62.6%	178	89.4%	137	90.7%
60,000 - 61,999	495	64.1%	452	67.1%	47	90.6%	51	91.9%
58,000 - 59,999	408	68.1%	362	70.8%	54	92.1%	39	92.9%
56,000 - 57,999	457	72.7%	453	75.3%	61	93.7%	79	94.9%
54,000 - 55,999	422	76.9%	446	79.8%	48	95.0%	30	95.6%
52,000 - 53,999	476	81.6%	414	84.0%	45	96.2%	43	96.7%
50,000 - 51,999	397	85.6%	358	87.6%	75	98.2%	55	98.0%
48,000 - 49,999	353	89.1%	321	90.9%	10	98.5%	11	98.3%
46,000 - 47,999	330	92.4%	263	93.5%	7	98.7%	33	99.1%
44,000 - 45,999	263	95.0%	220	95.7%	8	98.9%	5	99.2%
42,000 - 43,999	200	97.0%	170	97.5%	33	99.8%	16	99.6%
40,000 - 41,999	134	98.3%	124	98.7%	0	99.8%	6	99.8%
38,000 - 39,999	67	99.0%	46	99.2%	1	99.8%	2	99.8%
36,000 - 37,999	39	99.4%	32	99.5%	2	99.9%	3	99.9%
34,000 - 35,999	25	99.6%	17	99.7%	2	99.9%	2	100.0%
less than 34,000	36	100.0%	33	100.0%	2	100.0%	2	100.0%
Total Positions	**10,037**		**9,910**		**3,709**		**4,046**	
Median Salary	**66,260**		**68,407**		**95,020**		**95,046**	

TABLE 2: SALARY TRENDS IN ARL UNIVERSITY LIBRARIES

Salary figures for the current year are displayed in the context of previous years and compared to the changes in the US Consumer Price Index (CPI) to show trends in the purchasing power of median and beginning professional salaries. Salary figures and CPI numbers have been converted to adjusted indexes, using July 1984 as the base. Actual CPI data retrieved from the US Department of Labor, Bureau of Labor Statistics' *Consumer Price Index-All Urban Consumers (US All items, 1982–1984=100 - CUUR0000SA0)* available online at http://www.bls.gov/data/.

Note: Canadian salaries are expressed in US dollars.

Fiscal Year	Number of Libraries	Total Staff	Median Salary†	BPS‡ Median	Median Salary Index	BPS‡ Index	Actual CPI*	Adjusted CPI
2011–2012	115	9,910	$68,407	$46,000	262.1	278.8	225.9	217.4
2010–2011	115	10,037	66,260	44,004	253.9	266.7	218.0	209.8
2009–2010	114	10,207	64,560	43,700	247.4	264.8	215.4	207.3
2008–2009	113	10,148	64,823	44,000	248.4	266.7	219.9	211.6
2007–2008	113	9,983	61,833	41,125	236.9	249.7	208.3	200.5
2006–2007	113	9,824	59,648	40,000	228.5	242.4	203.5	195.9
2005–2006	113	9,655	57,074	37,920	218.7	229.8	195.4	188.1
2004–2005	113	9,487	55,250	36,984	211.7	224.1	189.4	182.3
2003–2004	114	9,492	53,000	36,000	203.1	218.2	183.9	177.0
2002–2003	114	9,469	51,636	35,000	197.8	212.1	180.1	173.3
2001–2002	113	9,198	50,724	34,000	194.3	206.1	177.5	170.8
2000–2001	112	8,882	49,068	32,879	188.0	199.3	172.8	166.3
1999-2000	111	8,595	47,377	31,100	181.5	188.5	166.7	160.4
1998–1999	110	8,400	45,775	30,000	175.2	181.7	163.2	157.1
1997–1998	110	8,414	44,534	28,500	170.5	172.6	160.5	154.5
1996–1997	109	8,325	43,170	27,687	165.3	167.7	157.0	151.1
1995–1996	108	8,231	41,901	27,000	160.5	163.6	152.5	146.8
1994–1995	108	8,216	41,088	26,000	157.4	157.6	148.4	142.8
1993–1994	108	8,132	40,225	25,834	154.1	156.6	144.4	139.0
1992–1993	108	8,212	39,265	25,000	150.4	151.5	140.5	134.9
1991–1992	107	8,256	38,537	24,000	147.7	145.5	136.2	131.1
1990–1991	107	8,382	36,701	23,800	140.6	144.2	130.4	125.8
1989–1990	107	8,253	34,629	22,000	132.7	133.3	124.4	119.3
1988–1989	107	8,087	32,461	20,400	124.4	123.6	118.5	113.9
1987–1988	106	7,962	30,534	19,460	117.0	117.9	113.8	109.3
1986–1987	105	7,718	28,941	18,250	110.9	110.6	109.5	105.5
1985–1986	105	7,543	27,485	17,500	105.3	106.1	107.8	103.6
1984–1985	104	7,161	26,100	16,500	100.0	100.0	104.1	100.0

*Actual CPI figures have been revised from previous editions based upon changes published by the Bureau of Labor Statistics. These changes are minute, less than 0.3 in all cases.
† Includes medical and law libraries.
‡ Beginning professional salary.

TABLE 3: SALARY TRENDS IN US ARL UNIVERSITY LIBRARIES

Salary figures for the current year are displayed in the context of previous years and compared to the changes in the US Consumer Price Index (CPI) to show trends in the purchasing power of median and beginning professional salaries. Salary figures and CPI numbers have been converted to adjusted indexes, using July 1984 as the base. Actual CPI data retrieved from the US Department of Labor, Bureau of Labor Statistics' *Consumer Price Index-All Urban Consumers (US All items, 1982–1984=100 - CUUR0000SA0)* available online at http://www.bls.gov/data/.

Fiscal Year	Number of Libraries	Total Staff	Median Salary†	Median Salary Change	Median Salary Index	Actual CPI*	Adjusted CPI	CPI Change
2011–2012	99	8,782	$66,467	2.3%	256.2	225.9	217.4	3.6%
2010–2011	99	8,925	65,000	1.5	250.5	218.0	209.8	1.2
2009–2010	99	9,116	64,069	0.6	246.9	215.4	207.3	-2.0
2008–2009	99	9,158	63,673	3.8	245.4	219.9	211.6	5.6
2007–2008	99	9,026	61,329	3.5	236.4	208.3	200.5	2.4
2006–2007	99	8,866	59,280	3.7	228.5	203.5	195.9	4.1
2005–2006	99	8,700	57,173	2.8	220.4	195.4	188.1	3.2
2004–2005	99	8,581	55,600	3.2	214.3	189.4	182.3	3.0
2003–2004	100	8,581	53,859	2.0	207.6	183.9	177.0	2.1
2002–2003	100	8,544	52,789	1.9	203.5	180.1	173.3	1.5
2001–2002	99	8,337	51,806	4.1	199.7	177.5	170.8	2.7
2000–2001	99	8,127	49,753	3.7	191.8	172.8	166.3	3.7
1999–2000	98	7,858	48,000	4.1	185.0	166.7	160.4	2.1
1998–1999	97	7,671	46,130	3.6	177.8	163.2	157.1	1.7
1997–1998	97	7,682	44,544	3.4	171.7	160.5	154.5	2.2
1996–1997	96	7,562	43,084	3.4	166.1	157.0	151.1	3.0
1995–1996	95	7,435	41,651	2.7	160.5	152.5	146.8	2.8
1994–1995	95	7,401	40,573	3.4	156.4	148.4	142.8	2.8
1993–1994	95	7,390	39,257	3.0	151.3	144.4	139.0	2.8
1992–1993	95	7,375	38,124	3.0	146.9	140.5	134.9	3.2
1991–1992	94	7,408	37,009	3.5	142.6	136.2	131.1	4.4
1990–1991	94	7,543	35,761	5.2	137.8	130.4	125.8	4.8
1989–1990	94	7,344	34,000	5.8	131.0	124.4	119.3	5.0
1988–1989	94	7,252	32,149	5.4	123.9	118.5	113.9	4.1
1987–1988	93	7,145	30,492	5.1	117.5	113.8	109.3	3.9
1986–1987	92	6,886	29,021	6.5	111.9	109.5	105.5	1.6
1985–1986	91	6,707	27,249	5.0	105.0	107.8	103.6	3.6
1984–1985	91	6,456	25,946	6.9	100.0	104.1	100.0	-

*Actual CPI figures have been revised from previous editions based upon changes published by the Bureau of Labor Statistics. These changes are minute, less than 0.3 in all cases.
† Includes medical and law libraries.

Table 4: Salary Trends in Canadian ARL University Libraries

Salary figures for the current year are displayed in the context of previous years. Canadian salaries are presented in both US $ and Canadian $ denominations and the annual exchange rate used in the salary surveys is also listed. Canadian salaries are also compared to the changes in the Canadian Consumer Price Index (CPI) to show trends in the purchasing power of median Canadian salaries. CPI number changes are based on July CPI figures. The source for Canadian CPI data is "Table 5: The Consumer Price Index for Canada" published in *The Daily*, a Statistics Canada publication, available online at http://www.statcan.gc.ca/pub/62-001-x/2011012/t040-eng.htm.

Fiscal Year	Number of Libraries	Total Staff	Median Salary in US $†	Median Salary Change†	Exchange Rate	Median Salary in Can. $	Median Salary Change	Can. CPI	Can. CPI Change*
2011–2012	16	1,128	$85,431	9.6%	1.00140	$85,551	4.0%	120.0	2.7%
2010–2011	16	1,112	77,919	12.7	1.0556	82,251	2.0	116.8	1.8
2009–2010	15	1,091	69,130	-11.3	1.1667	80,654	2.4	114.7	-0.9
2008–2009	14	990	77,954	15.8	1.0101	78,742	3.3	115.8	3.4
2007–2008	14	957	67,331	6.7	1.1323	76,239	3.9	112.0	2.2
2006–2007	14	958	63,112	11.8	1.16289	73,392	4.0	109.6	2.3
2005–2006	14	955	56,474	7.1	1.24971	70,576	-0.3	107.1	2.0
2004–2005	14	906	52,707	16.3	1.34328	70,800	3.5	105.0	2.3
2003–2004	14	911	45,310	6.2	1.51023	68,429	2.3	102.6	2.1
2002–2003	14	925	42,657	-0.6	1.56878	66,919	2.6	100.5	2.1
2001–2002	14	861	42,928	-1.1	1.51919	65,215	2.1	98.4	2.7
2000–2001	13	755	43,394	5.0	1.47192	63,873	2.4	95.8	2.9
1999-2000	13	737	41,316	-3.8	1.5103	62,400	2.4	93.1	1.9
1998–1999	13	729	42,963	-2.7	1.4177	60,909	0.9	91.4	1.0
1997–1998	13	732	44,167	1.4	1.3663	60,346	1.7	90.5	1.7
1996–1997	13	764	43,569	0.9	1.3613	59,310	-0.4	89.0	1.3
1995–1996	13	796	43,173	-1.7	1.3794	59,554	1.3	87.9	2.6
1994–1995	13	815	43,919	-6.0	1.3381	58,768	0.7	85.7	0.1
1993–1994	13	816	46,744	-4.3	1.2488	58,374	2.9	85.6	1.7
1992–1993	13	837	48,820	2.7	1.1623	56,744	3.4	84.2	1.2
1991–1992	13	847	47,519	5.5	1.1547	54,870	3.6	83.2	6.0
1990–1991	13	839	45,023	15.1	1.1759	52,942	12.5	78.5	4.1
1989–1990	13	853	39,117	12.3	1.2026	47,042	5.3	75.4	5.3
1988–1989	13	837	34,826	11.7	1.2826	44,668	5.3	71.6	3.9
1987–1988	13	817	31,178	10.9	1.3602	42,408	9.1	68.9	4.6
1986–1987	13	831	28,123	-1.9	1.3817	38,858	1.2	65.9	4.1
1985–1986	13	829	28,666	1.1	1.3388	38,378	7.9	63.3	4.1
1984–1985	12	705	28,346	-0.8	1.2548	35,569	0.8	60.8	4.1
Average				**4.3%**			**3.3%**		

† Includes medical and law libraries.

* Canadian CPI change figures have been revised from previous editions based upon changes published by *The Daily* (Statistics Canada). These changes were caused by rounding; they are minute and are less than 0.3 in all cases.

ARL Nonuniversity Libraries

Tables 5–6

TABLE 5: MEDIAN AND BEGINNING PROFESSIONAL SALARIES IN ARL NONUNIVERSITY LIBRARIES

	No. of Staff	Median Salaries		Beginning Salaries	
		FY 2010–2011	FY 2011–2012	FY 2010–2011	FY 2011–2012
Boston Public Library †	142	$67,267	$65,712	$40,975	$42,000
Canada Institute for Scientific and Technical Information *	76	73,649	77,923	53,155	57,370
Center for Research Libraries	32	52,179	53,411	33,878	34,680
Library & Archives Canada *	88	63,497	68,105	50,640	54,315
Library of Congress †	2,586	103,872	106,839	51,630	51,630
National Agricultural Library †	85	84,855	84,855	51,630	51,630
National Archives †	503	N/A	87,278	N/A	34,075
National Library of Medicine	202	92,341	92,341	42,209	42,209
New York Public Library †	221	61,438	61,633	42,638	42,638
New York State Library †	48	68,637	68,637	53,366	53,366
Smithsonian Library	63	87,350	72,876	51,630	51,630

* Canadian salaries are expressed in US dollars.
† See footnotes.

TABLE 6: SALARY TRENDS IN ARL NONUNIVERSITY LIBRARIES

Salary figures for the current year are displayed in the context of the previous years and compared to the changes in the Consumer Price Index (CPI) to show trends in the purchasing power of median and beginning professional salaries. Salary figures and CPI numbers have been converted to adjusted indexes, using July 1984 as the base. Actual CPI data retrieved from the US Department of Labor, Bureau of Labor Statistics' *Consumer Price Index-All Urban Consumers (US All items, 1982–1984=100 - CUUR0000SA0)* available online at http://www. bls.gov/data/.

Note: Canadian salaries are expressed in US dollars.

Fiscal Year	Number of Libraries	Total Staff	Median Salary	BPS† Median	Median Salary Index	BPS† Index	Actual CPI	Adjusted CPI
2011–2012	11	4,046	$95,046	$51,630	280.5	312.8	225.9	217.4
2010–2011	10	3,709	95,020	51,135	280.5	309.8	218.0	209.8
2009–2010	10	3,811	85,229	47,554	251.6	288.1	215.4	207.3
2008–2009	10	3,748	85,320	48,108	251.8	291.4	219.9	211.6
2007–2008	10	3,797	80,261	44,359	236.9	268.7	208.3	200.5
2006–2007	10	3,832	80,124	42,765	236.5	259.1	203.5	195.9
2005–2006	10	3,921	76,083	38,673	224.6	234.3	195.4	188.1
2004–2005	10	3,946	74,022	34,764	218.5	210.6	189.4	182.3
2003–2004	10	3,877	70,020	34,739	206.8	210.4	183.9	177.0
2002–2003	10	3,804	65,289	34,739	192.7	210.4	180.1	173.3
2001–2002	10	3,717	65,025	34,389	191.9	208.3	177.5	170.8
2000–2001	10	3,731	62,521	31,774	184.5	192.5	172.8	166.3
1999-2000	10	3,737	59,916	30,849	176.8	186.9	166.7	160.4
1998–1999	11	3,819	56,000	29,877	165.3	181.0	163.2	157.1
1997–1998	11	3,779	55,055	28,724	162.5	174.0	160.5	154.5
1996–1997	11	3,799	51,150	28,380	151.0	172.0	157.0	151.1
1995–1996	11	3,915	49,149	28,162	145.1	170.7	152.5	146.8
1994–1995	11	3,837	47,997	27,813	141.7	168.6	148.4	142.8
1993–1994	11	4,003	44,949	26,806	132.7	162.5	144.4	139.0
1992–1993	11	4,172	43,876	23,500	129.6	142.4	140.2	134.9
1991–1992	11	2,906	42,455	23,500	125.4	142.4	136.2	131.1
1990–1991	12	1,363	36,013	20,800	106.3	126.1	130.7	125.8
1989–1990	11	3,767	40,106	20,195	118.4	122.4	124.0	119.3
1988–1989	11	3,781	37,544	19,100	110.9	115.8	118.3	113.9
1987–1988	11	3,765	36,250	18,405	107.0	111.5	113.6	109.3
1986–1987	10	2,790	33,020	17,912	97.5	108.6	109.6	105.5
1985–1986	12	3,874	33,720	17,308	99.6	104.9	107.6	103.6
1984–1985	11	3,840	33,863	16,500	100.0	100.0	103.9	100.0

† Beginning professional salary.

ARL University Libraries

Tables 7–25

TABLE 7: FILLED POSITIONS; AVERAGE, MEDIAN, AND BEGINNING SALARIES; AND AVERAGE YEARS OF EXPERIENCE IN ARL UNIVERSITY LIBRARIES, FY 2011–2012

Institution	FILLED POSITIONS FY 2012	AVERAGE SALARIES FY 2011	AVERAGE SALARIES FY 2012	MEDIAN SALARIES FY 2011	MEDIAN SALARIES FY 2012	BEGINNING SALARIES FY 2011	BEGINNING SALARIES FY 2012	AVERAGE YRS. EXP. FY 2012
Alabama	59	$58,760	$62,893	$55,188	$60,146	$42,000	$42,000	15.1
Alberta‡	74	96,215	97,851	96,759	96,105	52,833	56,667	13.8
Arizona‡	46	65,351	68,992	59,118	61,977	50,857	53,364	18.6
Arizona State‡	55	64,744	64,394	65,039	63,390	43,000	43,000	19.7
Auburn‡	40	57,728	57,280	52,330	53,850	44,720	44,720	15.8
Boston University	58	59,680	61,525	57,200	61,600	33,000	33,000	18.1
Boston College‡	57	70,871	75,319	69,560	72,011	43,350	44,050	20.1
Brigham Young‡	102	67,295	69,291	66,000	68,350	52,020	53,060	19.0
British Columbia‡	80	85,029	92,321	83,131	90,375	52,420	55,258	17.3
Brown‡	69	66,368	68,427	62,972	62,503	40,500	55,000	19.2
Calgary‡	50	91,776	100,835	88,732	96,622	54,945	57,919	19.4
California, Berkeley‡	91	85,329	86,368	82,524	82,524	46,164	47,544	18.8
California, Davis‡	36	84,334	87,341	88,488	93,851	46,164	46,164	23.3
California, Irvine‡	44	77,825	79,022	75,708	78,506	46,144	46,164	17.7
California, Los Angeles‡	128	79,113	80,102	75,708	76,083	46,164	46,164	16.4
California, Riverside‡	45	79,762	80,107	79,116	79,116	47,087	48,029	21.4
California, San Diego‡	83	77,064	78,362	75,708	75,708	46,164	46,164	18.2
California, Santa Barbara‡	58	74,431	74,465	74,104	68,892	46,164	46,164	17.7
Case Western Reserve‡	42	58,886	61,443	55,434	57,709	35,000	35,700	16.8
Chicago‡	64	76,692	78,566	73,130	73,819	50,151	53,000	20.1
Cincinnati‡	61	68,451	68,279	66,260	65,591	42,000	43,000	19.8
Colorado‡	44	64,595	64,991	61,262	62,000	44,000	48,800	15.1
Colorado State‡	50	67,844	74,226	64,700	72,550	55,000	55,000	16.9
Columbia‡	200	74,360	76,368	65,280	67,660	52,000	53,600	16.3
Connecticut‡	64	81,341	79,448	79,309	78,073	50,000	50,000	17.2
Cornell‡	102	74,377	76,269	66,873	69,088	48,000	49,000	17.1
Dartmouth‡	50	70,594	72,320	67,159	68,724	45,500	45,500	17.6
Delaware	58	76,673	78,803	72,868	73,203	43,600	44,600	19.0
Duke‡	127	65,526	67,222	60,000	62,525	45,000	45,000	15.0
Emory‡	73	69,761	70,606	63,198	62,310	47,750	47,750	14.5
Florida‡	71	62,229	62,586	58,073	58,498	42,000	44,240	16.2
Florida State‡	38	56,313	56,750	52,265	52,711	42,000	42,000	12.4
George Washington‡	38	76,999	78,451	72,277	70,536	47,000	47,000	15.9
Georgetown‡	47	70,338	71,625	63,965	63,913	45,000	45,000	21.4
Georgia‡	74	56,057	56,671	49,795	50,000	38,000	38,000	17.1
Georgia Tech‡	46	63,534	61,398	58,016	60,000	44,000	46,000	14.8
Guelph‡	49	80,588	84,394	76,872	79,846	58,392	62,477	17.2
Harvard‡	438	79,111	83,106	72,134	77,371	53,093	59,691	16.3
Hawaii‡	79	63,037	65,023	64,692	65,346	35,000	35,000	16.2
Houston‡	47	62,188	63,580	54,628	57,884	44,000	48,000	14.3
Howard‡	13	56,590	59,723	50,223	52,764	34,627	48,000	23.4
Illinois, Chicago‡	37	63,420	66,915	57,730	61,983	47,000	47,000	18.3

Table 7: Filled Positions; Average, Median, and Beginning Salaries; and Average Years of Experience in ARL University Libraries, FY 2011–2012

Institution	Filled Positions FY 2012	Average Salaries		Median Salaries		Beginning Salaries		Average Yrs. Exp. FY 2012
		FY 2011	FY 2012	FY 2011	FY 2012	FY 2011	FY 2012	
Illinois, Urbana	125	69,964	72,020	65,129	66,929	50,000	51,500	15.6
Indiana[+]	75	63,918	65,490	59,331	60,613	40,400	40,400	18.6
Iowa[+]	61	64,501	66,758	57,840	61,669	41,000	43,000	20.3
Iowa State[+]	45	65,451	66,602	63,105	64,070	44,000	44,500	20.5
Johns Hopkins[+]	86	69,299	70,987	65,353	66,032	51,027	52,048	16.6
Kansas[+]	88	62,232	61,125	57,417	58,000	43,000	50,000	15.5
Kent State[+]	49	66,624	65,725	64,520	62,397	57,078	57,078	17.9
Kentucky[+]	66	60,762	62,691	59,984	62,036	41,000	41,000	22.6
Laval[+]	66	67,439	70,514	69,944	71,112	46,937	49,478	13.4
Louisiana State[+]	47	51,100	51,138	46,901	46,901	38,000	40,000	15.6
Louisville[+]	35	59,638	61,686	53,031	56,116	37,000	38,000	17.3
McGill[+]	55	71,450	74,171	64,865	66,178	47,366	49,930	15.5
McMaster[+]	42	69,041	73,274	62,118	66,313	45,945	48,388	17.3
Manitoba[+]	39	91,679	98,557	95,343	100,658	46,249	49,743	23.0
Maryland	70	69,981	72,077	69,035	68,847	40,000	40,000	21.9
Massachusetts[+]	57	72,957	73,609	73,553	75,102	42,155	43,750	18.9
MIT[+]	89	77,065	78,266	73,326	75,325	52,000	53,000	17.0
Miami[+]	59	69,503	67,051	65,000	63,787	45,000	45,000	15.6
Michigan[+]	147	71,354	72,094	65,884	67,920	42,000	43,500	17.0
Michigan State[+]	65	70,979	71,417	67,373	67,873	47,500	48,000	18.6
Minnesota	110	68,210	68,996	65,785	67,029	43,000	44,000	17.4
Missouri[+]	37	59,710	58,403	57,127	55,964	40,000	40,000	21.2
Montreal[+]	92	70,501	76,477	65,596	70,533	43,497	44,618	16.9
Nebraska	44	64,928	66,661	57,453	58,889	50,000	51,000	20.3
New Mexico[+]	46	71,159	70,710	67,913	66,163	40,000	40,000	19.9
New York University[+]	84	78,859	81,318	71,616	72,997	55,000	55,000	17.0
North Carolina	97	65,091	65,446	62,300	61,858	44,000	44,000	17.2
North Carolina State[+]	87	72,411	72,401	65,000	65,000	52,000	53,000	11.8
Northwestern[+]	92	68,146	67,168	62,995	62,266	44,000	44,000	14.9
Notre Dame[+]	59	71,751	74,569	67,915	70,705	44,000	44,000	19.6
Ohio University[+]	43	55,590	57,341	49,275	51,439	41,500	42,500	13.6
Ohio State[+]	115	57,846	60,435	53,292	54,336	46,000	46,000	13.7
Oklahoma[+]	43	55,299	56,361	53,477	54,870	42,000	42,000	14.5
Oklahoma State[+]	63	56,678	59,724	51,865	54,810	38,000	40,500	18.5
Oregon[+]	52	61,130	62,783	57,839	58,605	40,000	40,000	17.9
Ottawa[+]	38	87,360	89,246	85,122	88,111	47,538	50,111	16.9
Pennsylvania[+]	103	66,632	69,207	63,148	64,958	41,000	42,000	15.2
Pennsylvania State[+]	144	69,465	69,624	66,258	66,360	43,709	43,709	19.8
Pittsburgh[+]	65	69,211	71,385	62,897	63,996	34,000	34,000	20.7
Princeton[+]	110	82,454	84,500	76,100	79,000	63,200	64,400	21.9
Purdue[+]	58	65,562	74,559	61,006	67,068	47,000	49,500	18.9
Queen's[+]	33	96,157	105,943	99,005	109,110	50,446	53,842	22.4

Table 7: Filled Positions; Average, Median, and Beginning Salaries; and Average Years of Experience in ARL University Libraries, FY 2011–2012

Institution	Filled Positions FY 2012	Average Salaries FY 2011	Average Salaries FY 2012	Median Salaries FY 2011	Median Salaries FY 2012	Beginning Salaries FY 2011	Beginning Salaries FY 2012	Average Yrs. Exp. FY 2012
Rice	59	65,202	65,977	60,300	60,606	38,700	39,300	16.1
Rochester[+]	67	59,814	60,443	56,059	57,633	38,983	40,000	16.5
Rutgers[+]	85	91,176	90,975	91,751	91,735	50,765	50,765	23.0
Saskatchewan[+]	49	85,160	95,083	81,582	90,648	52,202	57,839	16.8
South Carolina[+]	47	52,032	53,874	48,627	50,852	38,000	38,000	15.6
Southern California[+]	109	76,057	78,811	69,761	71,282	48,500	48,500	19.9
Southern Illinois	31	59,157	60,429	56,912	58,032	44,000	44,000	15.6
SUNY Albany[+]	64	64,024	61,846	62,729	59,344	39,350	39,350	16.9
SUNY Buffalo[+]	63	75,265	78,098	70,554	75,000	47,000	47,000	21.4
SUNY Stony Brook[+]	19	87,447	88,464	79,599	80,895	43,000	45,000	20.6
Syracuse[+]	54	67,893	69,794	61,390	62,617	38,000	38,000	18.5
Temple[+]	39	69,082	70,498	60,048	61,978	44,004	44,044	20.1
Tennessee[+]	39	68,677	71,349	67,268	68,576	44,000	48,000	17.8
Texas[+]	118	66,964	65,075	59,304	58,000	45,000	46,000	16.0
Texas A&M[+]	98	64,966	63,266	59,055	58,092	48,500	48,500	14.7
Texas Tech[+]	67	58,352	60,816	54,163	57,936	45,000	49,000	12.3
Toronto	155	85,574	92,487	82,254	90,405	49,451	54,524	14.0
Tulane	35	62,835	65,668	59,492	61,979	40,000	40,000	18.9
Utah	57	61,061	64,334	55,375	58,588	45,000	45,000	19.1
Vanderbilt[+]	59	59,927	62,892	55,945	58,229	41,000	41,500	19.4
Virginia[+]	68	70,351	71,422	64,600	66,600	44,000	47,500	18.1
Virginia Tech[+]	36	63,308	62,578	58,540	59,040	40,000	40,000	17.1
Washington[+]	116	65,466	64,992	58,752	58,704	42,600	42,600	19.4
Washington State[+]	40	63,512	61,505	58,172	59,019	38,500	38,500	19.1
Washington U.–St. Louis[+]	63	60,832	61,093	55,489	55,690	40,000	40,000	17.4
Waterloo[+]	35	76,645	80,968	75,974	81,042	49,110	51,732	18.3
Wayne State[+]	45	60,697	61,219	55,396	58,200	41,000	41,000	15.4
Western Ontario[+]	62	68,581	75,958	66,961	74,991	47,836	53,925	14.0
Wisconsin[+]	148	61,068	60,592	57,692	57,385	40,526	40,526	17.6
Yale[+]	184	80,642	81,448	76,365	76,930	50,500	49,500	19.4
York	59	99,770	107,159	96,446	103,896	46,419	48,931	16.5

Excludes medical and law libraries. See Tables 35 and 42 for comparable figures for medical and law libraries.

Directors are included in figures for average years of experience and filled positions, but not in either the average or median salary statistics.

† Canadian salaries are expressed in US dollars.

‡ See Footnotes.

PAGE INTENTIONALLY LEFT BLANK.

TABLE 8: BEGINNING PROFESSIONAL SALARIES IN ARL UNIVERSITY LIBRARIES

RANK ORDER TABLE, FY 2010–2011

Rank	Institution	Salary	Rank	Institution	Salary
1	Princeton	63,200	59	Colorado	44,000
2	Guelph	58,392	59	Georgia Tech	44,000
3	Kent State	57,078	59	Houston	44,000
4	Colorado State	55,000	59	Iowa State	44,000
4	New York University	55,000	59	North Carolina	44,000
6	Calgary	54,945	59	Northwestern	44,000
7	Harvard	53,093	59	Notre Dame	44,000
8	Alberta	52,833	59	Southern Illinois	44,000
9	British Columbia	52,420	59	Tennessee	44,000
10	Saskatchewan	52,202	59	Virginia	44,000
11	Brigham Young	52,020	69	Pennsylvania State	43,709
12	Columbia	52,000	70	Delaware	43,600
12	MIT	52,000	71	Montreal	43,497
12	North Carolina State	52,000	72	Boston College	43,350
15	Johns Hopkins	51,027	73	Arizona State	43,000
16	Arizona	50,857	73	Kansas	43,000
17	Rutgers	50,765	73	Minnesota	43,000
18	Yale	50,500	73	SUNY Stony Brook	43,000
19	Queen's	50,446	77	Washington	42,600
20	Chicago	50,151	78	Massachusetts	42,155
21	Connecticut	50,000	79	Alabama	42,000
21	Illinois, Urbana	50,000	79	Cincinnati	42,000
21	Nebraska	50,000	79	Florida	42,000
24	Toronto	49,451	79	Florida State	42,000
25	Waterloo	49,110	79	Michigan	42,000
26	Southern California	48,500	79	Oklahoma	42,000
26	Texas A&M	48,500	85	Ohio University	41,500
28	Cornell	48,000	86	Iowa	41,000
29	Western Ontario	47,836	86	Kentucky	41,000
30	Emory	47,750	86	Pennsylvania	41,000
31	Ottawa	47,538	86	Vanderbilt	41,000
32	Michigan State	47,500	86	Wayne State	41,000
33	McGill	47,366	91	Wisconsin	40,526
34	California, Riverside	47,087	92	Brown	40,500
35	George Washington	47,000	93	Indiana	40,400
35	Illinois, Chicago	47,000	94	Maryland	40,000
35	Purdue	47,000	94	Missouri	40,000
35	SUNY Buffalo	47,000	94	New Mexico	40,000
39	Laval	46,937	94	Oregon	40,000
40	York	46,419	94	Tulane	40,000
41	Manitoba	46,249	94	Virginia Tech	40,000
42	California, Berkeley	46,164	94	Washington U.–St. Louis	40,000
42	California, Davis	46,164	101	SUNY Albany	39,350
42	California, Los Angeles	46,164	102	Rochester	38,983
42	California, San Diego	46,164	103	Rice	38,700
42	California, Santa Barbara	46,164	104	Washington State	38,500
47	California, Irvine	46,144	105	Georgia	38,000
48	Ohio State	46,000	105	Louisiana State	38,000
49	McMaster	45,945	105	Oklahoma State	38,000
50	Dartmouth	45,500	105	South Carolina	38,000
51	Duke	45,000	105	Syracuse	38,000
51	Georgetown	45,000	110	Louisville	37,000
51	Miami	45,000	111	Case Western Reserve	35,000
51	Texas	45,000	111	Hawaii	35,000
51	Texas Tech	45,000	113	Howard	34,627
51	Utah	45,000	114	Pittsburgh	34,000
57	Auburn	44,720	115	Boston University	33,000
58	Temple	44,004			

Reprinted from *ARL Annual Salary Survey 2010–2011*. Beginning salary figures represent officially designated base, not necessarily salaries of actual incumbents.

Excludes medical and law libraries. See Tables 36 and 43 for comparable figures for medical and law libraries.

Canadian salaries are expressed in US dollars.

TABLE 9: BEGINNING PROFESSIONAL SALARIES IN ARL UNIVERSITY LIBRARIES

RANK ORDER TABLE, FY 2011–2012

Rank	Institution	Salary	Rank	Institution	Salary
1	Princeton	64,400	57	Texas	46,000
2	Guelph	62,477	60	Dartmouth	45,500
3	Harvard	59,691	61	Duke	45,000
4	Calgary	57,919	61	Georgetown	45,000
5	Saskatchewan	57,839	61	Miami	45,000
6	Kent State	57,078	61	SUNY Stony Brook	45,000
7	Alberta	56,667	61	Utah	45,000
8	British Columbia	55,258	66	Auburn	44,720
9	Brown	55,000	67	Montreal	44,618
9	Colorado State	55,000	68	Delaware	44,600
9	New York University	55,000	69	Iowa State	44,500
12	Toronto	54,524	70	Florida	44,240
13	Western Ontario	53,925	71	Boston College	44,050
14	Queen's	53,842	72	Temple	44,044
15	Columbia	53,600	73	Minnesota	44,000
16	Arizona	53,364	73	North Carolina	44,000
17	Brigham Young	53,060	73	Northwestern	44,000
18	Chicago	53,000	73	Notre Dame	44,000
18	MIT	53,000	73	Southern Illinois	44,000
18	North Carolina State	53,000	78	Massachusetts	43,750
21	Johns Hopkins	52,048	79	Pennsylvania State	43,709
22	Waterloo	51,732	80	Michigan	43,500
23	Illinois, Urbana	51,500	81	Arizona State	43,000
24	Nebraska	51,000	81	Cincinnati	43,000
25	Rutgers	50,765	81	Iowa	43,000
26	Ottawa	50,111	84	Washington	42,600
27	Connecticut	50,000	85	Ohio University	42,500
27	Kansas	50,000	86	Alabama	42,000
29	McGill	49,930	86	Florida State	42,000
30	Manitoba	49,743	86	Oklahoma	42,000
31	Purdue	49,500	86	Pennsylvania	42,000
31	Yale	49,500	90	Vanderbilt	41,500
33	Laval	49,478	91	Kentucky	41,000
34	Cornell	49,000	91	Wayne State	41,000
34	Texas Tech	49,000	93	Wisconsin	40,526
36	York	48,931	94	Oklahoma State	40,500
37	Colorado	48,800	95	Indiana	40,400
38	Southern California	48,500	96	Louisiana State	40,000
38	Texas A&M	48,500	96	Maryland	40,000
40	McMaster	48,388	96	Missouri	40,000
41	California, Riverside	48,029	96	New Mexico	40,000
42	Houston	48,000	96	Oregon	40,000
42	Howard	48,000	96	Rochester	40,000
42	Michigan State	48,000	96	Tulane	40,000
42	Tennessee	48,000	96	Virginia Tech	40,000
46	Emory	47,750	96	Washington U.–St. Louis	40,000
47	California, Berkeley	47,544	105	SUNY Albany	39,350
48	Virginia	47,500	106	Rice	39,300
49	George Washington	47,000	107	Washington State	38,500
49	Illinois, Chicago	47,000	108	Georgia	38,000
49	SUNY Buffalo	47,000	108	Louisville	38,000
52	California, Davis	46,164	108	South Carolina	38,000
52	California, Irvine	46,164	108	Syracuse	38,000
52	California, Los Angeles	46,164	112	Case Western Reserve	35,700
52	California, San Diego	46,164	113	Hawaii	35,000
52	California, Santa Barbara	46,164	114	Pittsburgh	34,000
57	Georgia Tech	46,000	115	Boston University	33,000
57	Ohio State	46,000			

Beginning salary figures represent officially designated base, not necessarily salaries of actual incumbents.
Excludes medical and law libraries. See Tables 36 and 43 for comparable figures for medical and law libraries.
Canadian salaries are expressed in US dollars.

TABLE 10: MEDIAN PROFESSIONAL SALARIES IN ARL UNIVERSITY LIBRARIES
RANK ORDER TABLE, FY 2010–2011

Rank	Institution	Salary	Rank	Institution	Salary
1	Queen's	99,005	59	Kent State	64,520
2	Alberta	96,759	60	Georgetown	63,965
3	York	96,446	61	Emory	63,198
4	Manitoba	95,343	62	Pennsylvania	63,148
5	Rutgers	91,751	63	Iowa State	63,105
6	Calgary	88,732	64	Northwestern	62,995
7	California, Davis	88,488	65	Brown	62,972
8	Ottawa	85,122	66	Pittsburgh	62,897
9	British Columbia	83,131	67	SUNY Albany	62,729
10	California, Berkeley	82,524	68	North Carolina	62,300
11	Toronto	82,254	69	McMaster	62,118
12	Saskatchewan	81,582	70	Syracuse	61,390
13	SUNY Stony Brook	79,599	71	Colorado	61,262
14	Connecticut	79,309	72	Purdue	61,006
15	California, Riverside	79,116	73	Rice	60,300
16	Guelph	76,872	74	Temple	60,048
17	Yale	76,365	75	Duke	60,000
18	Princeton	76,100	76	Kentucky	59,984
19	Waterloo	75,974	77	Tulane	59,492
20	California, Irvine	75,708	78	Indiana	59,331
20	California, Los Angeles	75,708	79	Texas	59,304
20	California, San Diego	75,708	80	Arizona	59,118
23	California, Santa Barbara	74,104	81	Texas A&M	59,055
24	Massachusetts	73,553	82	Washington	58,752
25	MIT	73,326	83	Virginia Tech	58,540
26	Chicago	73,130	84	Washington State	58,172
27	Delaware	72,868	85	Florida	58,073
28	George Washington	72,277	86	Georgia Tech	58,016
29	Harvard	72,134	87	Iowa	57,840
30	New York University	71,616	88	Oregon	57,839
31	SUNY Buffalo	70,554	89	Illinois, Chicago	57,730
32	Laval	69,944	90	Wisconsin	57,692
33	Southern California	69,761	91	Nebraska	57,453
34	Boston College	69,560	92	Kansas	57,417
35	Maryland	69,035	93	Boston University	57,200
36	Notre Dame	67,915	94	Missouri	57,127
37	New Mexico	67,913	95	Southern Illinois	56,912
38	Michigan State	67,373	96	Rochester	56,059
39	Tennessee	67,268	97	Vanderbilt	55,945
40	Dartmouth	67,159	98	Washington U.–St. Louis	55,489
41	Western Ontario	66,961	99	Case Western Reserve	55,434
42	Cornell	66,873	100	Wayne State	55,396
43	Cincinnati	66,260	101	Utah	55,375
44	Pennsylvania State	66,258	102	Alabama	55,188
45	Brigham Young	66,000	103	Houston	54,628
46	Michigan	65,884	104	Texas Tech	54,163
47	Minnesota	65,785	105	Oklahoma	53,477
48	Montreal	65,596	106	Ohio State	53,292
49	Johns Hopkins	65,353	107	Louisville	53,031
50	Columbia	65,280	108	Auburn	52,330
51	Illinois, Urbana	65,129	109	Florida State	52,265
52	Arizona State	65,039	110	Oklahoma State	51,865
53	Miami	65,000	111	Howard	50,223
53	North Carolina State	65,000	112	Georgia	49,795
55	McGill	64,865	113	Ohio University	49,275
56	Colorado State	64,700	114	South Carolina	48,627
57	Hawaii	64,692	115	Louisiana State	46,901
58	Virginia	64,600			

Reprinted from *ARL Annual Salary Survey 2010–2011*. Salaries of directors are not included in the calculation of medians.
Excludes medical and law libraries. See Tables 37 and 44 for comparable figures for medical and law libraries.
Canadian salaries are expressed in US dollars.

TABLE 11: MEDIAN PROFESSIONAL SALARIES IN ARL UNIVERSITY LIBRARIES

RANK ORDER TABLE, FY 2011–2012

Rank	Institution	Salary	Rank	Institution	Salary
1	Queen's	109,110	59	Pennsylvania	64,958
2	York	103,896	60	Iowa State	64,070
3	Manitoba	100,658	61	Pittsburgh	63,996
4	Calgary	96,622	62	Georgetown	63,913
5	Alberta	96,105	63	Miami	63,787
6	California, Davis	93,851	64	Arizona State	63,390
7	Rutgers	91,735	65	Syracuse	62,617
8	Saskatchewan	90,648	66	Duke	62,525
9	Toronto	90,405	67	Brown	62,503
10	British Columbia	90,375	68	Kent State	62,397
11	Ottawa	88,111	69	Emory	62,310
12	California, Berkeley	82,524	70	Northwestern	62,266
13	Waterloo	81,042	71	Kentucky	62,036
14	SUNY Stony Brook	80,895	72	Colorado	62,000
15	Guelph	79,846	73	Illinois, Chicago	61,983
16	California, Riverside	79,116	74	Tulane	61,979
17	Princeton	79,000	75	Temple	61,978
18	California, Irvine	78,506	76	Arizona	61,977
19	Connecticut	78,073	77	North Carolina	61,858
20	Harvard	77,371	78	Iowa	61,669
21	Yale	76,930	79	Boston University	61,600
22	California, Los Angeles	76,083	80	Indiana	60,613
23	California, San Diego	75,708	81	Rice	60,606
24	MIT	75,325	82	Alabama	60,146
25	Massachusetts	75,102	83	Georgia Tech	60,000
26	SUNY Buffalo	75,000	84	SUNY Albany	59,344
27	Western Ontario	74,991	85	Virginia Tech	59,040
28	Chicago	73,819	86	Washington State	59,019
29	Delaware	73,203	87	Nebraska	58,889
30	New York University	72,997	88	Washington	58,704
31	Colorado State	72,550	89	Oregon	58,605
32	Boston College	72,011	90	Utah	58,588
33	Southern California	71,282	91	Florida	58,498
34	Laval	71,112	92	Vanderbilt	58,229
35	Notre Dame	70,705	93	Wayne State	58,200
36	George Washington	70,536	94	Texas A&M	58,092
37	Montreal	70,533	95	Southern Illinois	58,032
38	Cornell	69,088	96	Kansas	58,000
39	California, Santa Barbara	68,892	96	Texas	58,000
40	Maryland	68,847	98	Texas Tech	57,936
41	Dartmouth	68,724	99	Houston	57,884
42	Tennessee	68,576	100	Case Western Reserve	57,709
43	Brigham Young	68,350	101	Rochester	57,633
44	Michigan	67,920	102	Wisconsin	57,385
45	Michigan State	67,873	103	Louisville	56,116
46	Columbia	67,660	104	Missouri	55,964
47	Purdue	67,068	105	Washington U.–St. Louis	55,690
48	Minnesota	67,029	106	Oklahoma	54,870
49	Illinois, Urbana	66,929	107	Oklahoma State	54,810
50	Virginia	66,600	108	Ohio State	54,336
51	Pennsylvania State	66,360	109	Auburn	53,850
52	McMaster	66,313	110	Howard	52,764
53	McGill	66,178	111	Florida State	52,711
54	New Mexico	66,163	112	Ohio University	51,439
55	Johns Hopkins	66,032	113	South Carolina	50,852
56	Cincinnati	65,591	114	Georgia	50,000
57	Hawaii	65,346	115	Louisiana State	46,901
58	North Carolina State	65,000			

Salaries of directors are not included in the calculation of medians.

Excludes medical and law libraries. See Tables 37 and 44 for comparable figures for medical and law libraries.

Canadian salaries are expressed in US dollars.

Table 12: Average Professional Salaries in ARL University Libraries
Rank Order Table, FY 2010–2011

Rank	Institution	Salary	Rank	Institution	Salary
1	York	99,770	59	Northwestern	68,146
2	Alberta	96,215	60	Syracuse	67,893
3	Queen's	96,157	61	Colorado State	67,844
4	Calgary	91,776	62	Laval	67,439
5	Manitoba	91,679	63	Brigham Young	67,295
6	Rutgers	91,176	64	Texas	66,964
7	SUNY Stony Brook	87,447	65	Pennsylvania	66,632
8	Ottawa	87,360	66	Kent State	66,624
9	Toronto	85,574	67	Brown	66,368
10	California, Berkeley	85,329	68	Purdue	65,562
11	Saskatchewan	85,160	69	Duke	65,526
12	British Columbia	85,029	70	Washington	65,466
13	California, Davis	84,334	71	Iowa State	65,451
14	Princeton	82,454	72	Arizona	65,351
15	Connecticut	81,341	73	Rice	65,202
16	Yale	80,642	74	North Carolina	65,091
17	Guelph	80,588	75	Texas A&M	64,966
18	California, Riverside	79,762	76	Nebraska	64,928
19	California, Los Angeles	79,113	77	Arizona State	64,744
20	Harvard	79,111	78	Colorado	64,595
21	New York University	78,859	79	Iowa	64,501
22	California, Irvine	77,825	80	SUNY Albany	64,024
23	MIT	77,065	81	Indiana	63,918
24	California, San Diego	77,064	82	Georgia Tech	63,534
25	George Washington	76,999	83	Washington State	63,512
26	Chicago	76,692	84	Illinois, Chicago	63,420
27	Delaware	76,673	85	Virginia Tech	63,308
28	Waterloo	76,645	86	Hawaii	63,037
29	Southern California	76,057	87	Tulane	62,835
30	SUNY Buffalo	75,265	88	Kansas	62,232
31	California, Santa Barbara	74,431	89	Florida	62,229
32	Cornell	74,377	90	Houston	62,188
33	Columbia	74,360	91	Oregon	61,130
34	Massachusetts	72,957	92	Wisconsin	61,068
35	North Carolina State	72,411	93	Utah	61,061
36	Notre Dame	71,751	94	Washington U.–St. Louis	60,832
37	McGill	71,450	95	Kentucky	60,762
38	Michigan	71,354	96	Wayne State	60,697
39	New Mexico	71,159	97	Vanderbilt	59,927
40	Michigan State	70,979	98	Rochester	59,814
41	Boston College	70,871	99	Missouri	59,710
42	Dartmouth	70,594	100	Boston University	59,680
43	Montreal	70,501	101	Louisville	59,638
44	Virginia	70,351	102	Southern Illinois	59,157
45	Georgetown	70,338	103	Case Western Reserve	58,886
46	Maryland	69,981	104	Alabama	58,760
47	Illinois, Urbana	69,964	105	Texas Tech	58,352
48	Emory	69,761	106	Ohio State	57,846
49	Miami	69,503	107	Auburn	57,728
50	Pennsylvania State	69,465	108	Oklahoma State	56,678
51	Johns Hopkins	69,299	109	Howard	56,590
52	Pittsburgh	69,211	110	Florida State	56,313
53	Temple	69,082	111	Georgia	56,057
54	McMaster	69,041	112	Ohio University	55,590
55	Tennessee	68,677	113	Oklahoma	55,299
56	Western Ontario	68,581	114	South Carolina	52,032
57	Cincinnati	68,451	115	Louisiana State	51,100
58	Minnesota	68,210			

Reprinted from *ARL Annual Salary Survey 2010–2011*. Salaries of directors are not included in the calculation of averages.
Excludes medical and law libraries. See Tables 38 and 45 for comparable figures for medical and law libraries.
Canadian salaries are expressed in US dollars.

Table 13: Average Professional Salaries in ARL University Libraries

Rank Order Table, FY 2011–2012

Rank	Institution	Salary	Rank	Institution	Salary
1	York	107,159	59	Pennsylvania State	69,624
2	Queen's	105,943	60	Brigham Young	69,291
3	Calgary	100,835	61	Pennsylvania	69,207
4	Manitoba	98,557	62	Minnesota	68,996
5	Alberta	97,851	63	Arizona	68,992
6	Saskatchewan	95,083	64	Brown	68,427
7	Toronto	92,487	65	Cincinnati	68,279
8	British Columbia	92,321	66	Duke	67,222
9	Rutgers	90,975	67	Northwestern	67,168
10	Ottawa	89,246	68	Miami	67,051
11	SUNY Stony Brook	88,464	69	Illinois, Chicago	66,915
12	California, Davis	87,341	70	Iowa	66,758
13	California, Berkeley	86,368	71	Nebraska	66,661
14	Princeton	84,500	72	Iowa State	66,602
15	Guelph	84,394	73	Rice	65,977
16	Harvard	83,106	74	Kent State	65,725
17	Yale	81,448	75	Tulane	65,668
18	New York University	81,318	76	Indiana	65,490
19	Waterloo	80,968	77	North Carolina	65,446
20	California, Riverside	80,107	78	Texas	65,075
21	California, Los Angeles	80,102	79	Hawaii	65,023
22	Connecticut	79,448	80	Washington	64,992
23	California, Irvine	79,022	81	Colorado	64,991
24	Southern California	78,811	82	Arizona State	64,394
25	Delaware	78,803	83	Utah	64,334
26	Chicago	78,566	84	Houston	63,580
27	George Washington	78,451	85	Texas A&M	63,266
28	California, San Diego	78,362	86	Alabama	62,893
29	MIT	78,266	87	Vanderbilt	62,892
30	SUNY Buffalo	78,098	88	Oregon	62,783
31	Montreal	76,477	89	Kentucky	62,691
32	Columbia	76,368	90	Florida	62,586
33	Cornell	76,269	91	Virginia Tech	62,578
34	Western Ontario	75,958	92	SUNY Albany	61,846
35	Boston College	75,319	93	Louisville	61,686
36	Notre Dame	74,569	94	Boston University	61,525
37	Purdue	74,559	95	Washington State	61,505
38	California, Santa Barbara	74,465	96	Case Western Reserve	61,443
39	Colorado State	74,226	97	Georgia Tech	61,398
40	McGill	74,171	98	Wayne State	61,219
41	Massachusetts	73,609	99	Kansas	61,125
42	McMaster	73,274	100	Washington U.–St. Louis	61,093
43	North Carolina State	72,401	101	Texas Tech	60,816
44	Dartmouth	72,320	102	Wisconsin	60,592
45	Michigan	72,094	103	Rochester	60,443
46	Maryland	72,077	104	Ohio State	60,435
47	Illinois, Urbana	72,020	105	Southern Illinois	60,429
48	Georgetown	71,625	106	Oklahoma State	59,724
49	Virginia	71,422	107	Howard	59,723
50	Michigan State	71,417	108	Missouri	58,403
51	Pittsburgh	71,385	109	Ohio University	57,341
52	Tennessee	71,349	110	Auburn	57,280
53	Johns Hopkins	70,987	111	Florida State	56,750
54	New Mexico	70,710	112	Georgia	56,671
55	Emory	70,606	113	Oklahoma	56,361
56	Laval	70,514	114	South Carolina	53,874
57	Temple	70,498	115	Louisiana State	51,138
58	Syracuse	69,794			

Salaries of directors are not included in the calculation of averages.

Excludes medical and law libraries. See Tables 38 and 45 for comparable figures for medical and law libraries.

Canadian salaries are expressed in US dollars.

TABLE 14: AVERAGE, MEDIAN, AND BEGINNING PROFESSIONAL SALARIES IN ARL UNIVERSITY LIBRARIES SUMMARY OF RANKINGS, FYs 2008–2009 TO 2011–2012

Institution	Average Salaries				Median Salaries				Beginning Salaries			
FY	2009	2010	2011	2012	2009	2010	2011	2012	2009	2010	2011	2012
Alabama	97	103	104	86	105	108	102	82	73	72	79	86
Alberta	4	2	2	5	1	2	2	5	8	60	8	7
Arizona	65	63	72	63	62	70	80	76	26	16	16	16
Arizona State	77	60	77	82	66	42	52	64	60	61	73	81
Auburn	90	102	107	110	90	104	108	109	50	45	57	66
Boston University	40	105	100	94	91	84	93	79	70	57	115	115
Boston College	95	36	41	35	35	32	34	32	70	70	72	71
Brigham Young	72	61	63	60	60	48	45	43	22	7	11	17
British Columbia	10	26	12	8	9	25	9	10	2	21	9	8
Brown	53	64	67	64	51	62	65	67	99	100	92	9
Calgary	N/A	7	4	3	N/A	10	6	4	N/A	13	6	4
California, Berkeley	8	3	10	13	10	6	10	12	35	22	42	47
California, Davis	12	8	13	12	8	3	7	6	35	29	42	52
California, Irvine	20	19	22	23	16	12	20	18	35	29	47	52
California, Los Angeles	23	15	19	21	19	12	20	22	35	29	42	52
California, Riverside	26	16	18	20	18	12	15	16	27	22	34	41
California, San Diego	21	18	24	28	16	12	20	23	35	29	42	52
California, Santa Barbara	32	33	31	38	31	28	23	39	35	29	42	52
Case Western Reserve	98	101	103	96	96	97	99	100	110	111	111	112
Chicago	25	21	26	26	28	20	26	28	21	18	20	18
Cincinnati	60	67	57	65	64	57	43	56	100	92	79	81
Colorado	61	52	78	81	48	44	71	72	51	50	59	37
Colorado State	48	45	61	39	45	41	56	31	42	39	4	9
Columbia	31	28	33	32	49	45	50	46	4	5	12	15
Connecticut	11	5	15	22	12	8	14	19	22	19	21	27
Cornell	41	32	32	33	55	46	42	38	28	24	28	34
Dartmouth	30	31	42	44	30	30	40	41	67	37	50	60
Delaware	29	22	27	25	24	19	27	29	58	58	70	68
Duke	78	69	69	66	78	67	75	66	51	39	51	61
Emory	46	44	48	55	54	54	61	69	83	72	30	46
Florida	96	93	89	90	92	87	85	91	73	72	79	70
Florida State	113	111	110	111	113	111	109	111	73	72	79	86
George Washington	33	25	25	27	44	33	28	36	28	24	35	49
Georgetown	39	39	45	48	56	52	60	62	43	39	51	61
Georgia	99	107	111	112	106	109	112	114	105	104	105	108
Georgia Tech	86	73	82	97	86	80	86	83	73	50	59	57
Guelph	19	40	17	15	23	34	16	15	1	6	2	2
Harvard	16	17	20	16	25	23	29	20	18	15	7	3
Hawaii	54	57	86	79	33	38	57	57	65	66	111	113

TABLE 14: AVERAGE, MEDIAN, AND BEGINNING PROFESSIONAL SALARIES IN ARL UNIVERSITY LIBRARIES SUMMARY OF RANKINGS, FYs 2008–2009 TO 2011–2012

Institution	Average Salaries				Median Salaries				Beginning Salaries			
FY	2009	2010	2011	2012	2009	2010	2011	2012	2009	2010	2011	2012
Houston	75	84	90	84	59	85	103	99	73	61	59	42
Howard	110	114	109	107	101	114	111	110	108	104	113	42
Illinois, Chicago	83	81	84	69	85	86	89	73	28	24	35	49
Illinois, Urbana	57	56	47	47	61	61	51	49	41	34	21	23
Indiana	74	71	81	76	70	73	78	80	90	90	93	95
Iowa	76	78	79	70	83	96	87	78	85	83	86	81
Iowa State	80	74	71	72	74	60	63	60	60	61	59	69
Johns Hopkins	55	41	51	53	53	40	49	55	9	10	15	21
Kansas	85	90	88	99	87	98	92	96	16	7	73	27
Kent State	101	70	66	74	99	66	59	68	59	2	3	6
Kentucky	87	88	95	89	76	71	76	71	85	83	86	91
Laval	47	82	62	56	29	56	32	34	24	68	39	33
Louisiana State	112	113	115	115	112	113	115	115	105	104	105	96
Louisville	81	96	101	93	82	92	107	103	107	109	110	108
McGill	28	72	37	40	34	81	55	53	13	65	33	29
McMaster	14	85	54	42	11	55	69	52	49	91	49	40
Manitoba	3	6	5	4	2	4	4	3	33	81	41	30
Maryland	52	43	46	46	39	35	35	40	73	92	94	96
Massachusetts	35	35	34	41	21	21	24	25	72	71	78	78
MIT	24	24	23	29	25	22	25	24	6	4	12	18
Miami	45	46	49	68	46	59	53	63	43	39	51	61
Michigan	37	50	38	45	41	49	46	44	73	72	79	80
Michigan State	73	42	40	50	71	39	38	45	28	24	32	42
Minnesota	51	55	58	62	43	51	47	48	91	72	73	73
Missouri	106	94	99	108	110	91	94	104	91	92	94	96
Montreal	43	77	43	31	38	72	48	37	82	110	71	67
Nebraska	69	68	76	71	80	82	91	87	10	11	21	24
New Mexico	15	29	39	54	15	29	37	54	91	92	94	96
New York University	13	12	21	18	27	26	30	30	3	3	4	9
North Carolina	58	51	74	77	52	50	68	77	51	50	59	73
North Carolina State	34	27	35	43	47	43	53	58	16	11	12	18
Northwestern	66	49	59	67	57	53	64	70	73	61	59	73
Notre Dame	49	37	36	36	40	36	36	35	91	82	59	73
Ohio University	100	110	112	109	111	112	113	112	83	83	85	85
Ohio State	109	97	106	104	103	101	106	108	60	34	48	57
Oklahoma	108	108	113	113	104	102	105	106	73	72	79	86
Oklahoma State	104	106	108	106	100	106	110	107	108	104	105	94
Oregon	103	95	91	88	98	90	88	89	91	92	94	96
Ottawa	N/A	N/A	8	10	N/A	N/A	8	11	N/A	N/A	31	26

TABLE 14: AVERAGE, MEDIAN, AND BEGINNING PROFESSIONAL SALARIES IN ARL UNIVERSITY LIBRARIES SUMMARY OF RANKINGS, FYS 2008–2009 TO 2011–2012

Institution	Average Salaries				Median Salaries				Beginning Salaries			
FY	2009	2010	2011	2012	2009	2010	2011	2012	2009	2010	2011	2012
Pennsylvania	68	62	65	61	65	58	62	59	67	59	86	86
Pennsylvania State	42	48	50	59	42	47	44	51	69	69	69	79
Pittsburgh	63	58	52	51	73	63	66	61	111	112	114	114
Princeton	17	13	14	14	22	18	18	17	10	1	1	1
Purdue	59	66	68	37	66	65	72	47	43	24	35	31
Queen's	6	10	3	2	5	5	1	1	13	48	19	14
Rice	82	80	73	73	89	93	73	81	103	108	103	106
Rochester	105	109	98	103	102	105	96	101	104	103	102	96
Rutgers	5	1	6	9	3	1	5	7	25	14	17	25
Saskatchewan	7	20	11	6	7	7	12	8	12	38	10	5
South Carolina	111	112	114	114	108	110	114	113	111	112	105	108
Southern California	27	23	29	24	36	31	33	33	20	17	26	38
Southern Illinois	102	104	102	105	109	107	95	95	60	50	59	73
SUNY Albany	56	89	80	92	75	75	67	84	101	101	101	105
SUNY Buffalo	38	30	30	30	37	27	31	26	43	39	35	49
SUNY Stony Brook	22	11	7	11	20	16	13	14	51	72	73	61
Syracuse	71	65	60	58	63	64	70	65	113	N/A	105	108
Temple	67	54	53	57	88	79	74	75	64	49	58	72
Tennessee	36	38	55	52	32	37	39	42	51	50	59	42
Texas	62	53	64	78	77	74	79	96	43	34	51	57
Texas A&M	94	79	75	85	97	95	81	94	28	20	26	38
Texas Tech	88	91	105	101	93	83	104	98	43	39	51	34
Toronto	2	14	9	7	4	17	11	9	5	46	24	12
Tulane	79	92	87	75	71	88	77	74	91	92	94	96
Utah	84	86	93	83	81	89	101	90	51	50	51	61
Vanderbilt	92	100	97	87	94	100	97	92	91	88	86	90
Virginia	44	47	44	49	68	67	58	50	51	50	59	48
Virginia Tech	70	75	85	91	58	77	83	85	85	92	94	96
Washington	64	59	70	80	69	69	82	88	66	67	77	84
Washington State	91	76	83	95	84	78	84	86	101	102	104	107
Washington U.–St. Louis	93	99	94	100	95	103	98	105	91	92	94	96
Waterloo	18	34	28	19	13	24	19	13	15	47	25	22
Wayne State	107	87	96	98	107	99	100	93	89	88	86	91
Western Ontario	50	98	56	34	50	94	41	27	34	86	29	13
Wisconsin	89	83	92	102	79	76	90	102	88	87	91	93
Yale	9	9	16	17	14	11	17	21	7	9	18	31
York	1	4	1	1	6	9	3	2	19	80	40	36

Excludes medical and law libraries.

PAGE INTENTIONALLY LEFT BLANK.

Table 15: Distribution of Professional Staff in ARL University Libraries by Salary and Position, FY 2011–2012

Salary Intervals	Number of Staff								Percent at each level†							
	Dir.	Assoc. Dir.	Asst. Dir.	Branch Head	Subj. Spec.	Func. Spec.	Dept. Head	Other Prof.	Dir.	Assoc. Dir.	Asst. Dir.	Branch Head	Subj. Spec.	Func. Spec.	Dept. Head	Other Prof.
More than 300,000	7						1		6%						0%	
250,000–299,999	10								9%							
200,000–250,000	39	1	1	2					35%	0%	1%	0%				
175,000–199,999	29	9	2	1	3			1	26%	3%	1%	0%	0%			0%
150,000–174,999	23	30	8	8			4	2	21%	9%	5%	2%			0%	0%
140,000–149,999	2	24	5	7	5		7	2	2%	7%	3%	2%	0%		1%	0%
130,000–139,999	1	51	13	12	7	2	8	10	1%	16%	8%	3%	0%	0%	1%	0%
120,000–129,999		44	22	6	16	6	34	17		13%	14%	1%	1%	1%	3%	1%
110,000–119,999		76	18	24	26	24	63	34		23%	11%	6%	1%	2%	5%	1%
100,000–109,999	1	38	31	40	44	30	88	63	1%	12%	19%	9%	2%	3%	7%	2%
95,000–99,999		10	13	26	47	38	69	57		3%	8%	6%	2%	3%	5%	2%
90,000–94,999		14	17	34	73	21	85	47		4%	11%	8%	3%	2%	6%	2%
85,000–89,999		12	7	36	97	51	127	80		4%	4%	8%	5%	4%	10%	3%
80,000–84,999		11	5	42	135	62	146	109		3%	3%	10%	6%	5%	11%	4%
78,000–79,999		1	1	21	52	22	52	54		0%	1%	5%	2%	2%	4%	2%
76,000–77,999		1	1	11	60	42	52	52		0%	1%	3%	3%	4%	4%	2%
74,000–75,999		1	3	21	75	46	47	64		0%	2%	5%	4%	4%	4%	2%
72,000–73,999				29	88	41	55	82				7%	4%	4%	4%	3%
70,000–71,999		1		16	62	50	58	97		0%		4%	3%	4%	4%	4%
68,000–69,999			3	14	94	73	53	116			2%	3%	4%	6%	4%	4%
66,000–67,999		1		9	83	53	47	100		0%		2%	4%	5%	4%	4%
64,000–65,999			3	16	85	51	54	117			2%	4%	4%	4%	4%	5%
62,000–63,999			1	13	106	63	45	110			1%	3%	5%	5%	3%	4%
60,000–61,999		1		8	116	68	38	140		0%		2%	5%	6%	3%	5%
58,000–59,999			3	7	89	43	37	123			2%	2%	4%	4%	3%	5%
56,000–57,999			1	6	106	66	26	172			1%	1%	5%	6%	2%	7%
54,000–55,999			1	6	107	68	27	165			1%	1%	5%	6%	2%	6%
52,000–53,999			1	9	104	49	21	157			1%	2%	5%	4%	2%	6%
50,000–51,999				2	96	46	18	146				0%	4%	4%	1%	6%
48,000–49,999				3	106	60	15	102				1%	5%	5%	1%	4%
46,000–47,999				1	68	34	14	106				0%	3%	3%	1%	4%
44,000–45,999					65	26	4	83					3%	2%	0%	3%
42,000–43,999				1	52	15	9	64				0%	2%	1%	1%	2%
40,000–41,999				1	40	4	9	54				0%	2%	0%	1%	2%
38,000–39,999					11	1	2	24					1%		0%	1%
36,000–37,999				1	12	1	1	14				0%	1%		0%	1%
34,000–35,999					3	1	2	9					0%		0%	0%
less than 34,000					9	4	3	11					0%		0%	0%
Total	112	326	160	433	2142	1160	1321	2584	100%	100%	100%	100%	100%	100%	100%	100%

Excludes medical and law libraries.

† A "0" percentage indicates less than one–half of one percent.

Table 16: Distribution of Professional Staff in ARL University Libraries by Salary, Sex, and Position, FY 2011–2012

Salary Intervals	Women								Men							
	Dir.	Assoc. Dir.	Asst. Dir.	Branch Hd.	Subj. Spec.	Func. Spec.	Dept. Head	Other Prof.	Dir.	Assoc. Dir.	Asst. Dir.	Branch Hd.	Subj. Spec.	Func. Spec.	Dept. Head	Other Prof.
More than 300,000	2								5							
250,000 – 299,999	7								3							
200,000 – 250,000	29	1	1	1					10		1	1				
175,000 – 199,999	13	4	3	4	2				16	5	1	1	1		1	1
150,000 – 174,999	11	20	3	3			1	2	12	10	5	4			3	
140,000 – 149,999		14	3	7	3		4	2	1	10	2	5	2		3	
130,000 – 139,999	1	32	15	3	4	4	3	7		19	10	3	3	2	5	3
120,000 – 129,999		25	10	12	6	9	25	10		19	7	12	10	2	9	7
110,000 – 119,999	1	42	16	28	14	15	38	27		34	8	12	12	15	25	7
100,000 – 109,999		20	8	15	17	23	53	47		18	15	11	27	15	35	16
95,000 – 99,999		7	7	21	21	11	49	41		3	5	13	26	15	20	16
90,000 – 94,999		12	5	25	30	30	53	32		2	10	11	43	10	32	15
85,000 – 89,999		8		29	43	38	79	56		4	2	13	54	21	48	24
80,000 – 84,999		8	3	16	57	14	92	79		3	2	13	78	24	54	30
78,000 – 79,999				5	26	28	36	33		1	1	5	26	8	16	21
76,000 – 77,999			1	17	30	27	32	36		1		6	30	14	20	16
74,000 – 75,999		1	3	22	45	25	31	47				4	39	19	16	17
72,000 – 73,999				11	49	27	37	59				7	32	16	18	23
70,000 – 71,999				9	30	46	42	69				5	45	23	16	28
68,000 – 69,999			3	6	49	35	34	80		1		5	42	27	19	36
66,000 – 67,999				13	41	29	26	75				3	46	18	21	25
64,000 – 65,999			1	4	39	39	32	87		1	2	3	48	22	22	30
62,000 – 63,999			1	5	58	36	31	76				9	54	24	14	34
60,000 – 61,999		1		3	62	26	26	99				3	47	32	12	41
58,000 – 59,999			3	5	42	42	29	89				4	54	17	8	34
56,000 – 57,999			1	5	52	48	16	119				1	51	24	10	53
54,000 – 55,999				6	56	39	18	118			1	1	44	20	9	47
52,000 – 53,999			1	1	60	28	14	117				3	43	10	7	40
50,000 – 51,999				2	53	45	16	97				1	46	18	2	49
48,000 – 49,999				1	60	26	5	67					26	15	10	35
46,000 – 47,999					42	20	10	79					29	8	4	27
44,000 – 45,999					36	12	3	56					21	6	1	27
42,000 – 43,999				1	31	4	4	40				1	15	3	5	24
40,000 – 41,999					25		7	43					2	1	2	11
38,000 – 39,999					9	1		17					2		2	7
36,000 – 37,999					10	2	1	9					1		1	5
34,000 – 35,999					2		1	5						2	1	4
less than 34,000					4			8					5		2	3
Total	65	195	88	281	1108	729	848	1828	47	131	72	152	1034	431	473	756

Excludes medical and law libraries.

Table 17: Number and Average Salaries of ARL University Librarians by Position and Sex, FY 2011–2012

Position	Women Salary	Women No.	Men Salary	Men No.	Total Salary	Total No.
Director	$208,278	65	$209,492	47	$208,787	112
Associate Director	121,913	195	122,867	131	122,296	326
Assistant Director	104,851	88	114,372	72	109,135	160
Head, Branch	85,172	281	90,576	152	87,069	433
Functional Specialist	65,313	1,108	68,273	1,034	66,742	2,142
Subject Specialist	66,255	729	70,460	431	67,817	1,160
Dept. Head:						
Acquisitions	77,206	82	74,539	29	76,509	111
Reference	81,989	79	82,988	29	82,257	108
Cataloging	78,369	112	75,094	38	77,539	150
Serials	79,990	19	75,443	6	78,899	25
Documents/Maps	75,206	39	72,145	25	74,011	64
Circulation	75,190	56	65,545	30	71,825	86
Rare Books/Manuscripts	84,870	40	86,486	47	85,743	87
Computer Systems	97,072	19	93,642	45	94,660	64
Other	80,330	402	83,013	224	81,290	626
Reference:						
Over 14 years experience	73,274	384	73,672	168	73,395	552
10 to 14 years experience	64,417	152	63,333	66	64,089	218
5 to 9 years experience	59,121	182	57,809	70	58,757	252
Under 5 years experience	55,275	139	54,501	50	55,070	189
Cataloging:						
Over 14 years experience	68,795	258	68,424	117	68,679	375
10 to 14 years experience	61,584	79	63,616	32	62,170	111
5 to 9 years experience	58,842	91	57,878	41	58,542	132
Under 5 years experience	50,123	55	52,228	23	50,744	78
Other:						
Over 14 years experience	71,965	203	69,553	69	71,353	272
10 to 14 years experience	66,045	83	61,909	28	65,002	111
5 to 9 years experience	56,278	112	58,709	49	57,018	161
Under 5 years experience	52,706	90	51,541	43	52,329	133
All Positions	**$73,348**	**5,142**	**$76,225**	**3,096**	**$74,429**	**8,238**

Excludes medical and law libraries. See Tables 39 and 46 for comparable figures for medical and law libraries.
Canadian salaries are expressed in US dollars. See Table 32 for salaries of Canadian librarians expressed in Canadian dollars.

Table 18: Number and Average Years of Experience of ARL University Librarians by Position and Sex, FY 2011–2012

Position	Women Years	No.	Men Years	No.	Total Years	No.
Director	33.0	65	33.6	47	33.3	112
Associate Director	27.2	195	24.4	131	26.1	326
Assistant Director	24.3	88	22.8	72	23.6	160
Head, Branch	22.4	281	23.9	152	22.9	433
Functional Specialist	14.2	1,108	14.2	1,034	14.2	2,142
Subject Specialist	16.1	729	17.2	431	16.5	1,160
Dept. Head:						
Acquisitions	22.6	82	17.2	29	21.2	111
Reference	20.0	79	21.2	29	20.3	108
Cataloging	22.5	112	21.4	38	22.2	150
Serials	20.3	19	24.7	6	21.4	25
Documents/Maps	20.4	39	21.0	25	20.6	64
Circulation	19.7	56	17.1	30	18.8	86
Rare Books/Manuscripts	20.9	40	23.0	47	22.0	87
Computer Systems	20.9	19	18.3	45	19.1	64
Other	20.1	402	19.6	224	19.9	626
Public services	14.4	209	12.0	77	13.8	286
Technical services	15.3	127	12.0	58	14.3	185
Administration	15.7	152	14.4	54	15.4	206
Reference	15.5	857	15.8	354	15.6	1,211
Cataloger	17.6	483	18.4	213	17.8	696
All Positions	**17.5**	**5,142**	**17.3**	**3,096**	**17.4**	**8,238**

Excludes medical and law libraries. See Tables 40 and 47 for comparable figures for medical and law libraries.
Canadian salaries are expressed in US dollars. See Table 33 for salaries of Canadian librarians expressed in Canadian dollars.

TABLE 19: NUMBER AND AVERAGE SALARIES OF ARL UNIVERSITY LIBRARIANS BY YEARS OF EXPERIENCE AND SEX, FY 2011–2012

Experience	WOMEN		MEN		TOTAL		% OF TOTAL
	Salary	No.	Salary	No.	Salary	No.	
0–3 years	$53,360	438	$56,733	255	$54,601	693	8%
4–7 years	58,266	789	58,780	422	58,445	1,211	15%
8–11 years	64,345	691	66,565	467	65,240	1,158	14%
12–15 years	69,611	617	72,674	410	70,834	1,027	12%
16–19 years	74,418	507	76,944	324	75,403	831	10%
20–23 years	77,557	514	80,638	320	78,739	834	10%
24–27 years	83,103	479	88,899	271	85,197	750	9%
28–31 years	86,726	388	88,321	218	87,300	606	7%
32–35 years	91,167	328	98,890	202	94,110	530	6%
over 35 years	100,882	391	105,239	207	102,390	598	7%
All Positions	**$73,348**	**5,142**	**$76,225**	**3,096**	**$74,429**	**8,238**	**100%**

Excludes medical and law libraries. See Tables 41 and 48 for comparable figures for medical and law libraries.
Canadian salaries are expressed in US dollars. See Table 34 for salaries of Canadian librarians expressed in Canadian dollars.

TABLE 20: AVERAGE SALARIES OF ARL UNIVERSITY LIBRARIANS BY POSITION AND YEARS OF EXPERIENCE, FY 2011–2012

Position	YEARS OF EXPERIENCE									
	0–3 years	4–7 years	8–11 years	12–15 years	16–19 years	20–23 years	24–27 years	28–31 years	32–35 years	over 35 years
Director	‡	‡	.	.	‡	$215,818	$193,765	$217,533	$197,422	$212,140
Associate Director	.	$96,014	$106,728	$109,501	$114,368	120,720	133,313	122,589	121,824	131,932
Assistant Director	$107,733	94,390	90,790	98,989	110,413	110,521	110,819	111,369	115,165	120,595
Head, Branch	74,252	70,179	75,580	79,939	78,392	87,480	92,470	85,763	96,704	104,697
Functional Specialist	53,765	58,052	63,108	68,854	71,588	72,098	76,048	79,582	82,727	85,389
Subject Specialist	52,574	56,252	63,374	66,509	70,284	72,463	76,363	81,763	84,424	82,839
Dept. Head										
Acquisitions	‡	63,388	68,391	76,368	72,136	74,040	79,902	82,710	85,573	82,918
Reference	‡	69,094	73,039	83,418	76,295	84,051	82,572	86,356	99,849	101,748
Cataloging	‡	59,604	62,992	69,391	75,186	77,255	86,247	86,338	86,719	82,958
Serials	‡	.	72,874	‡	‡	72,091	‡	‡	‡	‡
Documents/Maps	65,523	50,014	60,867	80,348	77,868	73,943	71,324	80,842	‡	88,325
Circulation	59,363	55,910	58,843	71,145	90,185	73,618	72,700	86,815	91,280	80,689
Rare books	‡	73,571	83,049	74,829	75,657	89,013	93,817	75,882	89,681	104,395
Computer systems	.	95,447	98,561	89,196	97,530	85,046	‡	90,853	107,240	‡
Other	60,874	68,365	72,472	75,525	81,461	85,190	86,587	87,938	93,528	94,488
Public services	50,330	54,961	61,959	60,965	62,696	64,900	63,642	66,304	64,365	69,582
Technical services	48,249	51,577	60,030	60,404	67,917	67,611	68,330	65,225	82,055	74,678
Administration	59,353	59,835	64,761	71,456	67,366	80,483	81,120	87,757	86,012	96,943
Reference	54,778	56,779	63,487	65,184	67,599	71,014	74,990	75,321	76,926	80,946
Cataloger	50,092	56,399	59,625	63,791	63,655	65,045	69,718	73,055	71,851	72,765
All Positions:										
Average Salary	$54,601	$58,445	$65,240	$70,834	$75,403	$78,739	$85,197	$87,300	$94,110	$102,390
Number of Positions	693	1,211	1,158	1,027	831	834	750	606	530	598

Years of experience reflect total professional experience.
Excludes medical and law libraries.
Canadian salaries are expressed in US dollars.
‡ Salary data are not published when fewer than four individuals are involved.
. No positions reported in this category.

TABLE 21: NUMBER AND AVERAGE SALARIES OF ARL UNIVERSITY LIBRARIANS BY POSITION AND TYPE OF INSTITUTION, FY 2011–2012

Position	CANADIAN (16) Salary	No.	PRIVATE (31) Salary	No.	PUBLIC (68) Salary	No.	TOTAL (115) Salary	No.
Director	$184,797	16	$241,505	30	$199,731	66	$208,787	112
Associate Director	132,680	41	129,245	99	116,309	186	122,296	326
Assistant Director	106,448	19	111,546	80	106,811	61	109,135	160
Head, Branch	108,844	62	90,363	131	79,646	240	87,069	433
Functional Specialist	81,150	183	69,509	840	62,308	1,119	66,742	2,142
Subject Specialist	76,037	121	69,219	386	65,465	653	67,817	1,160
Dept. Head:								
Acquisitions	95,138	13	74,050	36	74,031	62	76,509	111
Reference	94,492	12	85,283	39	77,611	57	82,257	108
Cataloging	98,803	12	80,665	58	72,084	80	77,539	150
Serials	112,123	4	72,434	10	72,694	11	78,899	25
Documents/Maps	98,492	10	70,297	16	69,132	38	74,011	64
Circulation	85,985	13	69,474	27	69,203	46	71,825	86
Rare Books/Manuscripts	100,406	7	82,294	28	85,626	52	85,743	87
Computer Systems	102,884	8	92,265	18	94,064	38	94,660	64
Other	97,670	71	82,970	185	77,307	370	81,290	626
Reference:								
Over 14 years experience	99,005	98	68,596	154	67,493	300	73,395	552
10 to 14 years experience	81,551	45	63,442	53	57,826	120	64,089	218
5 to 9 years experience	78,777	62	56,887	57	50,225	133	58,757	252
Under 5 years experience	67,826	61	54,190	39	46,714	89	55,070	189
Cataloging:								
Over 14 years experience	89,155	29	69,961	154	64,558	192	68,679	375
10 to 14 years experience	84,507	7	64,383	60	55,598	44	62,170	111
5 to 9 years experience	77,625	11	61,343	62	52,041	59	58,542	132
Under 5 years experience	67,540	10	52,160	32	44,819	36	50,744	78
Other:								
Over 14 years experience	92,713	19	74,977	82	67,242	171	71,353	272
10 to 14 years experience	78,030	14	67,635	31	61,001	66	65,002	111
5 to 9 years experience	73,906	11	61,249	51	52,962	99	57,018	161
Under 5 years experience	64,730	19	54,952	34	48,269	80	52,329	133
All Positions	**$89,758**	**978**	**$76,019**	**2,792**	**$70,080**	**4,468**	**$74,429**	**8,238**

Excludes medical and law libraries.
Canadian salaries are expressed in US dollars. See Tables 31–34 for salaries of Canadian librarians expressed in Canadian dollars.
( ) Indicates the number of ARL libraries in each category.

TABLE 22: YEARS OF EXPERIENCE OF ARL UNIVERSITY LIBRARIANS BY POSITION AND TYPE OF INSTITUTION, FY 2011–2012

Position	CANADIAN (16) Years	No.	PRIVATE (31) Years	No.	PUBLIC (68) Years	No.	TOTAL (115) Years	No.
Director	33.6	16	33.1	30	33.2	66	33.3	112
Associate Director	23.5	41	26.9	99	26.2	186	26.1	326
Assistant Director	22.5	19	24.6	80	22.7	61	23.6	160
Head, Branch	21.9	62	22.8	131	23.3	240	22.9	433
Functional Specialist	14.4	183	14.1	840	14.2	1,119	14.2	2,142
Subject Specialist	13.7	121	17.3	386	16.6	653	16.5	1,160
Dept. Head:								
Acquisitions	19.3	13	20.4	36	22.1	62	21.2	111
Reference	16.2	12	21.4	39	20.4	57	20.3	108
Cataloging	23.9	12	22.8	58	21.6	80	22.2	150
Serials	23.8	4	22.6	10	19.4	11	21.4	25
Documents/Maps	19.4	10	21.2	16	20.7	38	20.6	64
Circulation	20.9	13	15.5	27	20.1	46	18.8	86
Rare Books/Manuscripts	22.0	7	21.0	28	22.5	52	22.0	87
Computer Systems	17.6	8	17.3	18	20.3	38	19.1	64
Other	20.1	71	19.8	185	19.9	370	19.9	626
Reference:								
Over 14 years experience	25.4	98	25.7	154	25.5	300	25.5	552
10 to 14 years experience	11.5	45	12.0	53	11.7	120	11.7	218
5 to 9 years experience	6.9	62	6.9	57	6.7	133	6.8	252
Under 5 years experience	2.4	61	2.7	39	2.6	89	2.6	189
Cataloging:								
Over 14 years experience	29.2	29	26.4	154	26.3	192	26.5	375
10 to 14 years experience	11.6	7	11.9	60	12.0	44	11.9	111
5 to 9 years experience	7.5	11	7.1	62	7.0	59	7.1	132
Under 5 years experience	1.8	10	2.5	32	2.9	36	2.6	78
Other:								
Over 14 years experience	26.1	19	25.4	82	25.8	171	25.7	272
10 to 14 years experience	11.6	14	11.7	31	12.0	66	11.9	111
5 to 9 years experience	6.2	11	6.8	51	6.8	99	6.7	161
Under 5 years experience	2.5	19	2.5	34	2.7	80	2.6	133
All Positions	**16.3**	**978**	**17.5**	**2,792**	**17.6**	**4,468**	**17.4**	**8,238**

Excludes medical and law libraries.
( ) Indicates the number of ARL libraries in each category.

Table 23: Number and Average Salaries of ARL University Librarians by Position and Size of Professional Staff, FY 2011–2012

Position	Staff Over 110 (13)† Salary	No.	Staff 75–110 (21) Salary	No.	Staff 50–74 (42) Salary	No.	Staff 13–49 (39)‡ Salary	No.
Director	$258,544	13	$221,661	21	$208,797	41	$183,989	37
Associate Director	138,800	59	122,956	83	117,975	112	114,732	72
Assistant Director	117,694	34	107,367	49	108,617	61	98,343	16
Head, Branch	92,391	116	89,063	95	83,400	147	83,505	75
Functional Specialist	69,427	664	68,663	506	64,572	659	62,507	313
Subject Specialist	70,295	318	69,508	298	65,670	387	64,884	157
Dept. Head:								
Acquisitions	73,876	19	84,678	18	74,524	45	76,245	29
Reference	88,472	21	84,589	20	79,322	34	79,913	33
Cataloging	81,493	41	84,884	28	71,483	48	75,205	33
Serials	74,067	9	75,626	5	92,128	4	79,888	7
Documents/Maps	86,146	13	72,741	11	76,784	22	62,633	18
Circulation	79,314	19	75,361	14	66,957	32	70,110	21
Rare Books/Manuscripts	97,852	10	95,154	17	78,583	33	84,083	27
Computer Systems	103,674	9	100,517	14	87,323	24	95,424	17
Other	83,486	149	86,038	148	77,237	200	79,589	129
Reference:								
Over 14 years experience	72,414	97	75,115	111	71,122	181	75,332	163
10 to 14 years experience	66,102	43	65,319	52	63,874	64	61,769	59
5 to 9 years experience	63,409	41	61,736	58	58,798	81	53,661	72
Under 5 years experience	59,705	42	56,033	35	55,590	70	48,768	42
Cataloging:								
Over 14 years experience	76,442	106	66,753	102	64,049	114	66,821	53
10 to 14 years experience	68,247	42	58,845	28	58,106	20	58,321	21
5 to 9 years experience	65,975	51	55,936	29	52,728	33	52,670	19
Under 5 years experience	55,470	16	49,039	23	51,904	24	46,460	15
Other:								
Over 14 years experience	75,005	77	74,227	67	70,375	68	64,565	60
10 to 14 years experience	71,188	36	62,300	29	65,940	22	58,127	24
5 to 9 years experience	56,223	54	58,686	42	59,060	33	54,065	32
Under 5 years experience	52,702	46	52,961	39	53,987	24	48,930	24
All Positions	**$75,974**	**2,145**	**$75,910**	**1,942**	**$73,167**	**2,583**	**$72,562**	**1,568**

Excludes medical and law libraries.

Canadian salaries are expressed in US dollars. See Tables 31–34 for salaries of Canadian librarians expressed in Canadian dollars.

( ) Indicates the number of ARL libraries in each category.

† In 1995–1996 and earlier, the first column of this table reported staff over 124; in 1996–1998 over 120; in 1998–1999 over 115; and since 1999–2000, over 110.

‡ No ARL library has fewer than 13 professional staff members.

TABLE 24: YEARS OF EXPERIENCE OF ARL UNIVERSITY LIBRARIANS BY POSITION AND SIZE OF PROFESSIONAL STAFF, FY 2011–2012

Position	STAFF OVER 110 (13)[†]		STAFF 75–110 (21)		STAFF 50–74 (42)		STAFF 13–49 (39)[‡]	
	Years	No.	Years	No.	Years	No.	Years	No.
Director	30.8	13	34.4	21	32.6	41	34.1	37
Associate Director	25.2	59	26.2	83	25.7	112	27.3	72
Assistant Director	22.5	34	23.2	49	24.8	61	22.6	16
Head, Branch	23.2	116	22.8	95	22.5	147	23.4	75
Functional Specialist	13.8	664	14.3	506	14.0	659	15.2	313
Subject Specialist	15.6	318	16.9	298	17.5	387	15.3	157
Dept. Head:								
Acquisitions	19.1	19	23.5	18	21.9	45	20.1	29
Reference	21.9	21	21.6	20	19.7	34	19.2	33
Cataloging	20.4	41	24.8	28	22.8	48	21.5	33
Serials	23.7	9	19.6	5	24.5	4	17.9	7
Documents/Maps	23.5	13	19.2	11	24.0	22	15.2	18
Circulation	20.5	19	16.8	14	18.7	32	18.7	21
Rare Books/Manuscripts	19.1	10	23.9	17	20.6	33	23.6	27
Computer Systems	21.6	9	18.1	14	18.7	24	19.2	17
Other	21.4	149	20.1	148	19.3	200	19.0	129
Reference:								
Over 14 years experience	25.0	97	26.2	111	25.4	181	25.5	163
10 to 14 years experience	11.9	43	11.4	52	12.2	64	11.3	59
5 to 9 years experience	7.1	41	6.9	58	6.8	81	6.5	72
Under 5 years experience	2.4	42	2.5	35	2.5	70	2.8	42
Cataloging:								
Over 14 years experience	27.8	106	25.2	102	27.0	114	25.7	53
10 to 14 years experience	11.8	42	11.8	28	12.0	20	12.2	21
5 to 9 years experience	6.9	51	7.3	29	7.0	33	7.3	19
Under 5 years experience	2.9	16	2.3	23	2.7	24	2.8	15
Other:								
Over 14 years experience	26.4	77	25.0	67	25.7	68	25.5	60
10 to 14 years experience	12.2	36	12.1	29	11.7	22	11.4	24
5 to 9 years experience	6.7	54	6.8	42	6.7	33	6.8	32
Under 5 years experience	2.7	46	2.7	39	2.7	24	2.2	24
All Positions	**16.7**	**2,145**	**17.4**	**1,942**	**17.8**	**2,583**	**17.8**	**1,568**

Excludes medical and law libraries.

( ) Indicates the number of ARL libraries in each category.

† In 1995–1996 and earlier, the first column of this table reported staff over 124; in 1996–1998 over 120; in 1998–1999 over 115; and since 1999–2000, over 110.

‡ No ARL library has fewer than 13 professional staff members.

Table 25: Average Salaries of ARL University Librarians by Position and Geographic Region, FY 2011–2012

Position	Northeast — New England (9)	Northeast — Middle Atlantic (14)	North Central — East North Central (17)	North Central — West North Central (7)	South — South Atlantic (18)	South — East South Central (6)	South — West South Central (9)	West — Mountain (7)	West — Pacific (12)	Canada (16)	Total (115)
Director	$229,301	$247,361	$214,536	$195,153	$220,703	$185,950	$197,572	$186,493	$200,933	$184,797	$208,787
Associate Director	131,715	129,290	116,630	112,389	125,873	110,081	101,772	114,877	125,363	132,680	122,296
Assistant Director	107,497	120,482	93,195	101,057	111,344		104,476	114,638	102,298	106,448	109,135
Head, Branch	97,380	90,590	79,344	76,681	75,410	78,603	77,726	84,422	83,462	108,844	87,069
Functional Specialist	75,549	67,392	60,876	64,127	62,532	54,331	57,105	64,576	69,460	81,150	66,742
Subject Specialist	75,466	70,631	64,404	61,567	59,511	58,537	55,836	62,739	74,791	76,037	67,817
Dept. Head:											
Acquisitions	82,665	77,679	72,404	69,296	71,862	66,207	69,064	80,366	77,383	95,138	76,509
Reference	95,070	85,210	73,618	74,560	79,264	70,820	69,477	82,313	83,582	94,492	82,257
Cataloging	91,017	78,163	72,937	72,025	67,279	63,438	67,599	76,305	84,800	98,803	77,539
Serials	‡	‡	72,261	.	70,520	‡	‡	‡	‡	112,123	78,899
Documents/Maps	81,102	72,537	71,901	69,353	59,868	‡	67,440	67,054	‡	98,492	74,011
Circulation	74,285	72,644	71,852	55,758	72,972	‡	61,247	‡	76,994	85,985	71,825
Rare Books/Manuscripts	89,622	93,241	88,995	73,842	88,710	74,876	80,110	78,182	76,502	100,406	85,743
Computer Systems	109,891	94,368	85,679	‡	97,053	81,837	106,822	88,441	94,986	102,884	94,660
Other	86,003	84,297	78,413	65,291	75,009	73,648	67,761	72,137	92,845	97,670	81,290
Reference:											
Over 14 years experience	74,585	71,344	67,745	58,337	65,209	64,624	56,308	63,469	72,294	99,005	73,395
10 to 14 years experience	68,387	61,243	58,783	53,655	58,196	58,931	49,836	56,637	59,869	81,551	64,089
5 to 9 years experience	61,990	53,470	53,751	52,942	51,913	49,646	48,072	47,756	49,781	78,777	58,757
Under 5 years experience	58,749	52,073	47,401	46,462	48,824	45,028	39,512	47,044	47,430	67,826	55,070
Cataloging:											
Over 14 years experience	79,072	66,200	61,343	59,776	60,456	60,290	56,237	64,937	73,062	89,155	68,679
10 to 14 years experience	70,155	61,052	54,657	51,163	52,749	‡	55,637	57,333	60,310	84,507	62,170
5 to 9 years experience	66,339	57,838	52,903	48,819	49,994	46,689	48,736	‡	56,340	77,625	58,542
Under 5 years experience	57,057	46,454	45,140	‡	45,799	43,838	‡	‡	44,782	67,540	50,744
Other:											
Over 14 years experience	78,213	77,709	68,648	57,662	64,210	72,439	55,105	64,320	77,919	92,713	71,353
10 to 14 years experience	71,784	65,807	62,189	52,849	59,757	‡	61,575	52,980	70,707	78,030	65,002
5 to 9 years experience	68,293	56,345	52,005	54,927	53,283	52,395	53,825	53,541	58,474	73,906	57,018
Under 5 years experience	60,312	55,256	45,818	56,135	52,303	‡	47,679	53,835	45,969	64,730	52,329
All Positions											
Average Salary	$79,946	$76,648	$69,306	$66,735	$69,755	$65,532	$64,036	$70,255	$76,666	$89,758	$74,429
Number of Positions	1,066	1,199	1,256	448	1,135	298	577	400	881	978	8,238

Excludes medical and law libraries.
Canadian salaries are expressed in US dollars.
( ) Indicates number of ARL libraries included.
‡ Salary data are not published when fewer than four individuals are involved.

ARL University Libraries by Geographic Region

Region	Number of Libraries	ARL University Libraries Included	States/Provinces Included
Northeast			
1. New England	9	Boston University, Boston College, Brown, Connecticut, Dartmouth, Harvard, Massachusetts Institute of Technology, Massachusetts, Yale	Conn., Mass., Me., N.H., R.I., Vt.
2. Middle Atlantic	14	Columbia; Cornell; New York; Pennsylvania; Pennsylvania State; Pittsburgh; Princeton; Rochester; Rutgers; State University of New York: Albany, Buffalo, Stony Brook; Syracuse; Temple	N.J., N.Y., Pa.
North Central			
3. East North Central	17	Case Western Reserve, Chicago, Cincinnati, Illinois–Chicago, Illinois–Urbana, Indiana, Kent State, Michigan, Michigan State, Notre Dame, Northwestern, Ohio University, Ohio State, Purdue, Southern Illinois, Wayne State, Wisconsin	Ill., Ind., Mich., Ohio, Wis.
4. West North Central	7	Iowa, Iowa State, Kansas, Minnesota, Missouri, Nebraska, Washington U.–St. Louis	Iowa, Kan., Minn., Mo., Neb., N. Dak., S. Dak.
South			
5. South Atlantic	18	Delaware, Duke, Emory, Florida, Florida State, Georgia, Georgia Tech., Georgetown, George Washington, Howard, Johns Hopkins, Maryland, Miami, North Carolina, North Carolina State, South Carolina, Virginia, Virginia Tech	Del., DC, Fla., Ga., Md., N.C., S.C., Va., W. Va.
6. East South Central	6	Alabama, Auburn, Kentucky, Louisville, Tennessee, Vanderbilt	Ala., Ky., Miss., Tenn.
7. West South Central	9	Houston, Louisiana State, Oklahoma, Oklahoma State, Rice, Texas, Texas A&M, Texas Tech, Tulane	Ark., La., Okla., Tex.
West			
8. Mountain	7	Arizona, Arizona State, Brigham Young, Colorado, Colorado State, New Mexico, Utah	Ariz., Colo., Idaho, Mont., Nev., N. Mex., Utah, Wyo.
9. Pacific	12	University of California: Berkeley, Davis, Irvine, Los Angeles, Riverside, San Diego, Santa Barbara; Hawaii; Oregon; Southern California; Washington; Washington State	Alaska, Calif., Hawaii, Ore., Wash.
Canada	16	Alberta, British Columbia, Calgary, Guelph, Laval, McGill, McMaster, Manitoba, Montreal, Ottawa, Queen's, Saskatchewan, Toronto, Waterloo, Western Ontario, York	Alta., B.C., Man., N. Br., Newf., N.S., Ont., P.E.I., Que., Sask.

Regions are based on the classification used by the US Bureau of the Census in tabulations of the Current Population Survey.

US ARL University Libraries

Tables 26–30

TABLE 26: AVERAGE SALARIES OF US ARL UNIVERSITY LIBRARIANS BY POSITION AND YEARS OF EXPERIENCE, FY 2011–2012

Position	0–3 years	4–7 years	8–11 years	12–15 years	16–19 years	20–23 years	24–27 years	28–31 years	32–35 years	over 35 years
Director	‡	‡	.	.	‡	$223,494	$203,174	$227,246	$199,811	$214,207
Associate Director	.	‡	$96,802	$109,770	$113,307	120,242	129,692	121,203	121,192	130,848
Assistant Director	‡	$94,390	90,819	98,989	110,004	115,004	112,380	111,333	116,264	119,533
Head, Branch	$71,915	63,601	71,000	77,737	75,223	85,421	86,555	82,540	95,301	98,744
Functional Specialist	52,440	56,488	62,235	67,537	69,804	71,015	73,772	78,746	80,778	85,374
Subject Specialist	51,869	54,772	61,999	65,480	69,670	71,143	75,422	79,468	82,519	80,949
Dept. Head:										
Acquisitions	‡	63,388	63,718	69,330	71,382	72,557	76,061	78,957	85,938	82,918
Reference	‡	61,556	70,915	82,137	76,028	83,624	80,182	86,356	94,961	98,771
Cataloging	‡	59,604	62,992	68,466	73,153	75,249	83,680	82,726	86,719	82,958
Serials	‡	.	64,126	‡	‡	72,091	.	‡	‡	‡
Documents/Maps	‡	50,014	60,867	‡	67,118	69,005	71,324	80,842	.	82,073
Circulation	55,514	55,637	58,843	69,511	90,185	66,168	73,640	82,108	‡	80,684
Rare Books/Manuscripts	‡	‡	78,363	74,065	75,657	86,772	92,973	75,882	89,681	104,809
Computer Systems	.	‡	98,561	90,205	96,479	85,545	‡	90,853	107,240	.
Other	57,909	65,651	69,685	73,946	80,804	82,330	83,846	85,708	91,733	93,397
Public services	47,654	53,698	60,025	60,125	60,876	64,900	64,822	66,304	64,365	69,582
Technical services	46,551	50,174	58,641	59,906	62,314	63,149	67,032	61,018	82,055	74,678
Administration	58,367	57,283	63,796	69,156	67,366	77,173	83,942	87,757	86,650	84,827
Reference	48,735	50,345	58,144	60,234	62,021	64,741	68,399	71,757	74,072	73,039
Cataloger	46,982	55,274	57,014	62,749	63,034	64,962	67,572	71,204	69,035	69,480
All Positions										
Average Salary	$52,376	$55,877	$62,971	$69,073	$73,503	$76,407	$81,863	$85,319	$92,709	$99,745
Number of Positions	559	1,058	1,024	922	754	742	649	548	475	529

Excludes Canadian libraries.
Excludes medical and law libraries.
‡ Salary data are not published when fewer than four individuals are involved.
. No positions reported in this category.

TABLE 27: NUMBER AND AVERAGE SALARIES OF MINORITY US ARL UNIVERSITY LIBRARIANS BY POSITION AND SEX, FY 2011–2012

Position	WOMEN Salary	No.	MEN Salary	No.	TOTAL Salary	No.
Director	‡	6	‡	2	$185,297	8
Associate Director	$122,327	15	$137,043	7	127,010	22
Assistant Director	110,798	7	120,027	7	115,412	14
Head, Branch	71,220	28	88,839	12	76,506	40
Functional Specialist	62,367	142	68,994	122	65,429	264
Subject Specialist	64,782	157	67,516	60	65,538	217
Dept. Head:						
Acquisitions	‡	10	‡	1	68,920	11
Reference	82,313	8	.		82,313	8
Cataloging	‡	21	‡	2	74,317	23
Serials	‡	2	.		‡	2
Documents/Maps	‡	3	‡	1	68,809	4
Circulation	‡	3	‡	5	74,263	8
Rare Books/Manuscripts	80,687	5	.		80,687	5
Computer Systems	‡	3	‡	5	85,303	8
Other	82,607	36	74,402	17	79,975	53
Reference:						
Over 14 years experience	69,521	38	69,084	14	69,403	52
10 to 14 years experience	54,264	13	61,372	9	57,171	22
5 to 9 years experience	54,173	27	55,457	5	54,373	32
Under 5 years experience	49,165	21	48,878	7	49,094	28
Cataloging:						
Over 14 years experience	63,873	41	72,941	11	65,791	52
10 to 14 years experience	59,145	11	63,214	5	60,417	16
5 to 9 years experience	57,551	21	54,683	7	56,834	28
Under 5 years experience	‡	12	‡	2	50,008	14
Other:						
Over 14 years experience	69,190	15	66,931	5	68,625	20
10 to 14 years experience	‡	8	‡	1	62,855	9
5 to 9 years experience	‡	19	‡	3	56,483	22
Under 5 years experience	48,690	16	44,897	5	47,787	21
All Positions	**$67,048**	**688**	**$71,825**	**315**	**$68,548**	**1,003**

Excludes Canadian libraries.
Excludes medical and law libraries.
‡ Salary data are not published when fewer than four individuals are involved in either category.
. No positions reported in this category.

TABLE 28: NUMBER AND AVERAGE YEARS OF EXPERIENCE OF MINORITY US ARL UNIVERSITY LIBRARIANS BY POSITION AND SEX, FY 2011–2012

Position	WOMEN		MEN		TOTAL	
	Years	No.	Years	No.	Years	No.
Director	24.2	6	43.5	2	29.0	8
Associate Director	29.8	15	20.7	7	26.9	22
Assistant Director	26.0	7	16.0	7	21.0	14
Head, Branch	19.7	28	23.6	12	20.9	40
Functional Specialist	13.6	142	14.2	122	13.9	264
Subject Specialist	14.3	157	13.9	60	14.2	217
Dept. Head:						
Acquisitions	14.9	10	5.0	1	14.0	11
Reference	24.8	8	.		24.8	8
Cataloging	20.5	21	25.0	2	20.9	23
Serials	14.0	2	.		14.0	2
Documents/Maps	13.3	3	14.0	1	13.5	4
Circulation	9.3	3	19.8	5	15.9	8
Rare Books/Manuscripts	17.6	5	.		17.6	5
Computer Systems	20.0	3	16.6	5	17.9	8
Other	21.1	36	20.4	17	20.9	53
Public services	10.9	27	13.7	3	11.2	30
Technical services	10.7	18	3.4	5	9.1	23
Administration	14.3	13	14.0	6	14.2	19
Reference	13.9	99	14.1	35	13.9	134
Cataloger	16.2	85	15.2	25	16.0	110
All Positions	**15.6**	**688**	**15.3**	**315**	**15.5**	**1,003**

Excludes Canadian libraries. See Table 33 for comparable figures for Canadian libraries.
Excludes medical and law libraries. See Tables 40 and 47 for comparable figures for medical and law libraries.
. No positions reported in this category.

TABLE 29: NUMBER AND AVERAGE SALARIES OF US ARL UNIVERSITY LIBRARIANS BY YEARS OF EXPERIENCE AND SEX, FY 2011–2012

Experience	WOMEN		MEN		TOTAL		% OF TOTAL
	Salary	No.	Salary	No.	Salary	No.	
0–3 years	$50,615	343	$55,173	216	$52,376	559	8%
4–7 years	55,369	675	56,773	383	55,877	1,058	15%
8–11 years	61,534	599	64,995	425	62,971	1,024	14%
12–15 years	67,617	551	71,236	371	69,073	922	13%
16–19 years	72,087	456	75,669	298	73,503	754	10%
20–23 years	75,185	454	78,332	288	76,407	742	10%
24–27 years	79,734	418	85,716	231	81,863	649	9%
28–31 years	84,484	346	86,750	202	85,319	548	8%
32–35 years	89,407	293	98,025	182	92,709	475	7%
over 35 years	97,888	337	103,004	192	99,745	529	7%
All Positions	**$71,020**	**4,472**	**$74,520**	**2,788**	**$72,364**	**7,260**	**100%**

Excludes Canadian libraries.
Excludes medical and law libraries.

TABLE 30: NUMBER AND AVERAGE SALARIES OF MINORITY US ARL UNIVERSITY LIBRARIANS BY YEARS OF EXPERIENCE AND SEX, FY 2011–2012

Experience	WOMEN Salary	No.	MEN Salary	No.	TOTAL Salary	No.	% OF TOTAL
0–3 years	$50,745	66	$58,185	28	$52,961	94	9%
4–7 years	55,831	136	57,487	52	56,289	188	19%
8–11 years	60,209	106	68,819	57	63,220	163	16%
12–15 years	65,286	71	73,156	56	68,756	127	13%
16–19 years	73,813	84	73,700	28	73,785	112	11%
20–23 years	75,846	71	79,348	31	76,910	102	10%
24–27 years	79,112	51	83,506	15	80,111	66	7%
28–31 years	73,488	29	81,027	17	76,275	46	5%
32–35 years	78,631	32	84,395	15	80,471	47	5%
over 35 years	92,905	42	97,974	16	94,303	58	6%
All Positions	**$67,048**	**688**	**$71,825**	**315**	**$68,548**	**1,003**	**100%**

Excludes Canadian libraries.
Excludes medical and law libraries.

Canadian ARL University Libraries

Tables 31–34

TABLE 31: FILLED POSITIONS; AVERAGE, MEDIAN, AND BEGINNING PROFESSIONAL SALARIES; AND AVERAGE YEARS OF PROFESSIONAL EXPERIENCE IN CANADIAN ARL UNIVERSITY LIBRARIES, FY 2011–2012

Institution	FILLED POSITIONS FY 2012	AVERAGE SALARIES		MEDIAN SALARIES		BEGINNING SALARIES		AVERAGE YRS. EXP.
		FY 2011	FY 2012	FY 2011	FY 2012	FY 2011	FY 2012	FY 2012
Alberta‡	74	$101,564	$97,988	$102,139	$96,240	$55,770	$56,746	13.8
British Columbia‡	80	89,757	92,450	87,753	90,502	55,335	55,335	17.3
Calgary‡	50	96,879	100,976	93,666	96,757	58,000	58,000	19.4
Guelph‡	49	85,069	84,513	81,146	79,958	61,639	62,564	17.2
Laval‡	66	71,189	70,613	73,833	71,212	49,547	49,547	13.4
McGill‡	55	75,422	74,275	68,471	66,271	50,000	50,000	15.5
McMaster‡	42	72,880	73,376	65,572	66,406	48,500	48,456	17.3
Manitoba‡	39	96,777	98,695	100,644	100,799	48,820	49,813	23.0
Montreal‡	92	74,421	76,584	69,243	70,632	45,915	44,680	16.9
Ottawa‡	38	92,217	89,371	89,855	88,234	50,181	50,181	16.9
Queen's‡	33	101,504	106,091	104,510	109,263	53,251	53,917	22.4
Saskatchewan‡	49	89,895	95,216	86,118	90,775	55,104	57,920	16.8
Toronto	155	90,332	92,617	86,827	90,532	52,200	54,600	14.0
Waterloo‡	35	80,906	81,082	80,198	81,156	51,840	51,804	18.3
Western Ontario‡	62	72,394	76,064	70,684	75,096	50,496	54,000	14.0
York	59	105,317	107,309	101,808	104,041	49,000	49,000	16.5

Salaries are expressed in Canadian dollars.

Excludes Canadian medical and law libraries. See Tables 35 and 42 for comparable figures for medical and law libraries.

Directors are included in figures for average years of experience and filled positions, but not in either the average or median salary statistics.

‡ See Footnotes.

Table 32: Number and Average Salaries of Canadian ARL University Librarians by Position and Sex, FY 2011–2012

Position	Women Salary	Women No.	Men Salary	Men No.	Total Salary	Total No.
Director	$190,669	9	$177,839	7	$185,056	16
Associate Director	132,945	26	132,727	15	132,865	41
Assistant Director	109,440	12	101,725	7	106,598	19
Head, Branch	109,815	50	105,588	12	108,997	62
Functional Specialist	78,091	91	84,401	92	81,263	183
Subject Specialist	74,018	83	80,787	38	76,144	121
Dept. Head:						
Acquisitions	‡	12	‡	1	95,271	13
Reference	‡	11	‡	1	94,624	12
Cataloging	‡	10	‡	2	98,941	12
Serials	‡	3	‡	1	112,280	4
Documents/Maps	‡	7	‡	3	98,630	10
Circulation	‡	11	‡	2	86,106	13
Rare Books/Manuscripts	‡	4	‡	3	100,546	7
Computer Systems	‡	3	‡	5	103,028	8
Other	97,242	49	99,066	22	97,807	71
Reference:						
Over 14 years experience	97,842	69	102,242	29	99,144	98
10 to 14 years experience	83,656	33	76,189	12	81,665	45
5 to 9 years experience	78,057	49	82,019	13	78,888	62
Under 5 years experience	67,107	49	71,244	12	67,921	61
Cataloging:						
Over 14 years experience	88,326	21	91,782	8	89,279	29
10 to 14 years experience	‡	5	‡	2	84,626	7
5 to 9 years experience	‡	9	‡	2	77,734	11
Under 5 years experience	‡	8	‡	2	67,635	10
Other:						
Over 14 years experience	92,846	14	92,832	5	92,842	19
10 to 14 years experience	‡	12	‡	2	78,139	14
5 to 9 years experience	74,856	6	72,995	5	74,010	11
Under 5 years experience	65,698	14	62,364	5	64,821	19
All Positions	**$89,008**	**670**	**$91,790**	**308**	**$89,884**	**978**

Salaries are expressed in Canadian dollars.

Excludes Canadian medical and law libraries. See Tables 39 and 46 for comparable figures for medical and law libraries.

† Salary data are not published when fewer than four individuals are involved in either category.

. No positions reported in this category.

Table 33: Number and Average Years of Experience of Canadian ARL University Librarians by Position and Sex, FY 2011–2012

Position	Women		Men		Total	
	Years	No.	Years	No.	Years	No.
Director	34.6	9	32.4	7	33.6	16
Associate Director	24.3	26	22.2	15	23.5	41
Assistant Director	23.3	12	21.1	7	22.5	19
Head, Branch	22.4	50	19.6	12	21.9	62
Functional Specialist	13.3	91	15.6	92	14.4	183
Subject Specialist	13.5	83	14.2	38	13.7	121
Dept. Head:						
Acquisitions	20.0	12	11.0	1	19.3	13
Reference	14.6	11	33.0	1	16.2	12
Cataloging	23.4	10	26.5	2	23.9	12
Serials	20.3	3	34.0	1	23.8	4
Documents / Maps	22.4	7	12.3	3	19.4	10
Circulation	23.4	11	7.5	2	20.9	13
Rare Books / Manuscripts	19.0	4	26.0	3	22.0	7
Computer Systems	22.3	3	14.8	5	17.6	8
Other	20.6	49	19.2	22	20.1	71
Public services	8.5	17	5.6	7	7.7	24
Technical services	14.6	7	14.4	7	14.5	14
Administration	16.1	22	11.0	3	15.5	25
Reference	13.1	200	14.4	66	13.4	266
Cataloger	17.2	43	20.6	14	18.1	57
All Positions	**16.3**	**670**	**16.5**	**308**	**16.3**	**978**

Excludes Canadian medical and law libraries. See Tables 40 and 47 for comparable figures for medical and law libraries.
. No positions reported in this category.

TABLE 34: NUMBER AND AVERAGE SALARIES OF CANADIAN ARL UNIVERSITY LIBRARIANS BY YEARS OF EXPERIENCE AND SEX, FY 2011–2012

Experience	WOMEN Salary	No.	MEN Salary	No.	TOTAL Salary	No.	% OF TOTAL
0–3 years	$63,361	95	$65,463	39	$63,973	134	14%
4–7 years	75,521	114	78,609	39	76,308	153	16%
8–11 years	82,759	92	82,567	42	82,699	134	14%
12–15 years	86,376	66	86,478	39	86,414	105	11%
16–19 years	95,389	51	91,685	26	94,139	77	8%
20–23 years	95,636	60	101,535	32	97,688	92	9%
24–27 years	106,339	61	107,433	40	106,772	101	10%
28–31 years	105,346	42	108,313	16	106,164	58	6%
32–35 years	106,054	35	106,908	20	106,364	55	6%
over 35 years	119,734	54	134,036	15	122,843	69	7%
All Positions	**$89,008**	**670**	**$91,790**	**308**	**$89,884**	**978**	**100%**

Salaries are expressed in Canadian dollars
Excludes Canadian medical and law libraries. See Tables 41 and 48 for comparable figures for medical and law libraries.

ARL University Medical Libraries

Tables 35–41

TABLE 35: FILLED POSITIONS; AVERAGE, MEDIAN, AND BEGINNING SALARIES; AND AVERAGE YEARS OF EXPERIENCE IN ARL UNIVERSITY MEDICAL LIBRARIES, FY 2011–2012

Institution	Filled Positions	Average Salary	Median Salary	Beginning Salary	Average Yrs. Exp.
Alabama	2	‡	‡	$42,000	17.5
Alberta	6	$95,367	$113,249	56,667	17.7
Arizona	16	64,591	57,208	51,500	20.1
Boston	12	57,155	52,750	47,000	8.7
British Columbia	11	85,576	87,323	55,258	20.5
Calgary	11	80,754	73,772	57,919	12.5
California, Davis	5	61,875	64,560	46,164	21.0
California, Los Angeles	12	78,309	82,524	46,164	20.3
California, San Diego	9	70,200	75,708	46,164	13.7
Case Western Reserve	7	68,651	72,471	35,700	28.9
Cincinnati	15	59,994	51,440	43,000	21.9
Columbia	10	70,645	75,279	53,600	16.4
Connecticut	15	79,605	77,974	56,454	18.5
Cornell	10	80,939	81,373	60,000	19.2
Dartmouth	8	63,819	66,595	45,500	19.4
Duke	19	59,946	56,897	48,000	16.2
Emory	12	64,211	59,095	48,000	17.8
Florida	14	55,320	48,746	50,000	13.9
Florida State	5	52,637	53,883	40,000	15.0
George Washington	13	68,038	67,985	48,000	17.5
Georgetown	11	62,958	63,456	44,000	14.7
Harvard	59	83,012	77,307	59,691	6.6
Hawaii	2	‡	‡	45,000	24.5
Howard	9	69,500	66,000	60,000	15.6
Illinois, Chicago	19	62,734	58,737	47,000	15.2
Iowa	9	67,896	59,287	43,000	21.1
Johns Hopkins	23	71,580	71,073	45,000	16.0
Kansas	10	51,616	47,500	43,000	15.0
Kentucky	13	57,661	56,855	41,000	24.5
Louisiana State	1	‡	‡	36,000	6.0
Louisville	10	57,677	53,374	38,000	21.1
McGill	9	77,530	74,842	49,930	19.0
McMaster	8	75,773	82,721	48,388	14.1
Manitoba	19	79,413	79,073	49,743	15.8
Miami	11	74,087	70,529	45,000	14.8
Michigan	17	63,455	62,108	43,500	15.6
Minnesota	15	63,278	63,379	44,000	17.3
Missouri	10	53,740	50,533	40,000	20.6
Montreal	10	75,236	70,533	54,076	21.0
Nebraska	14	65,518	59,376	45,000	21.4
New York	24	70,081	64,000	55,000	11.5
North Carolina	28	69,174	65,860	45,000	21.0

TABLE 35: FILLED POSITIONS; AVERAGE, MEDIAN, AND BEGINNING SALARIES; AND AVERAGE YEARS OF EXPERIENCE IN ARL UNIVERSITY MEDICAL LIBRARIES, FY 2011–2012

Institution	Filled Positions	Average Salary	Median Salary	Beginning Salary	Average Yrs. Exp.
Northwestern	17	67,350	67,825	51,000	17.9
Ohio State	10	67,779	65,149	46,000	19.0
Oklahoma	8	63,050	61,690	40,000	21.1
Oklahoma State	4	53,968	49,500	38,000	24.0
Ottawa	7	85,060	79,586	50,111	15.3
Pennsylvania	11	65,042	61,180	45,000	18.6
Pennsylvania State	7	62,662	62,982	45,000	14.7
Pittsburgh	27	62,134	60,030	45,000	16.0
Queen's	7	90,715	86,848	53,842	17.4
Rochester	25	58,325	54,326	40,000	20.9
Saskatchewan	7	79,311	78,931	57,839	10.4
South Carolina	9	49,291	46,692	35,000	15.1
Southern California	15	74,170	70,072	51,500	18.0
Southern Illinois	5	63,036	66,247	41,000	25.4
Suny–Buffalo	14	68,934	65,833	47,000	22.4
Suny–Stony Brook	18	73,018	72,686	45,000	16.7
Temple	8	59,147	58,331	42,800	20.6
Tennessee – Knoxville	4	‡	‡	38,000	15.0
Tennessee – Memphis	12	54,145	54,918	56,000	20.3
Texas Tech	23	49,315	45,634	38,110	20.2
Toronto	14	98,963	98,960	54,524	17.1
Tulane	8	54,850	50,184	40,000	15.3
Utah	18	64,626	61,000	40,000	20.0
Vanderbilt	14	66,991	69,738	41,500	14.6
Virginia	15	65,786	65,600	45,000	22.7
Washington	18	64,655	59,040	42,600	19.7
Washington U.–St. Louis	23	63,365	54,675	40,000	19.9
Wayne State	4	‡	‡	45,600	20.8
Wisconsin	15	60,472	55,491	40,526	16.2
Yale	20	78,346	76,000	49,500	17.8

Directors are included in figures for filled positions and average years of experience, but not in either the average or median salary statistics. Canadian salaries are expressed in US dollars.

‡ Salary data are not published when fewer than four individuals are involved.

TABLE 36: BEGINNING PROFESSIONAL SALARIES IN ARL UNIVERSITY MEDICAL LIBRARIES RANK ORDER TABLE, FY 2011–2012

Rank	Institution	Salary	Rank	Institution	Salary
1	Cornell	60,000	36	Johns Hopkins	45,000
1	Howard	60,000	36	Miami	45,000
3	Harvard	59,691	36	Nebraska	45,000
4	Calgary	57,919	36	North Carolina	45,000
5	Saskatchewan	57,839	36	Pennsylvania	45,000
6	Alberta	56,667	36	Pennsylvania State	45,000
7	Connecticut	56,454	36	Pittsburgh	45,000
8	Tennessee, Memphis	56,000	36	SUNY Stony Brook	45,000
9	British Columbia	55,258	36	Virginia	45,000
10	New York University	55,000	46	Georgetown	44,000
11	Toronto	54,524	46	Minnesota	44,000
12	Montreal	54,076	48	Michigan	43,500
13	Queen's	53,842	49	Cincinnati	43,000
14	Columbia	53,600	49	Iowa	43,000
15	Arizona	51,500	49	Kansas	43,000
15	Southern California	51,500	52	Temple	42,800
17	Northwestern	51,000	53	Washington	42,600
18	Ottawa	50,111	54	Alabama	42,000
19	Florida	50,000	55	Vanderbilt	41,500
20	McGill	49,930	56	Kentucky	41,000
21	Manitoba	49,743	56	Southern Illinois	41,000
22	Yale	49,500	58	Wisconsin	40,526
23	McMaster	48,388	59	Florida State	40,000
24	Duke	48,000	59	Missouri	40,000
24	Emory	48,000	59	Oklahoma	40,000
24	George Washington	48,000	59	Rochester	40,000
27	Boston University	47,000	59	Tulane	40,000
27	Illinois, Chicago	47,000	59	Utah	40,000
27	SUNY Buffalo	47,000	59	Washington U.–St. Louis	40,000
30	California, Davis	46,164	66	Texas Tech	38,110
30	California, Los Angeles	46,164	67	Louisville	38,000
30	California, San Diego	46,164	67	Oklahoma State	38,000
33	Ohio State	46,000	67	Tennessee, Knoxville	38,000
34	Wayne State	45,600	70	Louisiana State	36,000
35	Dartmouth	45,500	71	Case Western Reserve	35,700
36	Hawaii	45,000	72	South Carolina	35,000

Beginning salary figures represent officially designated base, not necessarily salaries of actual incumbents.
Canadian salaries are expressed in US dollars.

TABLE 37: MEDIAN PROFESSIONAL SALARIES IN ARL UNIVERSITY MEDICAL LIBRARIES RANK ORDER TABLE, FY 2011–2012

Rank	Institution	Salary	Rank	Institution	Salary
1	Alberta	113,249	37	Minnesota	63,379
2	Toronto	98,960	38	Pennsylvania State	62,982
3	British Columbia	87,323	39	Michigan	62,108
4	Queen's	86,848	40	Oklahoma	61,690
5	McMaster	82,721	41	Pennsylvania	61,180
6	California, Los Angeles	82,524	42	Utah	61,000
7	Cornell	81,373	43	Pittsburgh	60,030
8	Ottawa	79,586	44	Nebraska	59,376
9	Manitoba	79,073	45	Iowa	59,287
10	Saskatchewan	78,931	46	Emory	59,095
11	Connecticut	77,974	47	Washington	59,040
12	Harvard	77,307	48	Illinois, Chicago	58,737
13	Yale	76,000	49	Temple	58,331
14	California, San Diego	75,708	50	Arizona	57,208
15	Columbia	75,279	51	Duke	56,897
16	McGill	74,842	52	Kentucky	56,855
17	Calgary	73,772	53	Wisconsin	55,491
18	SUNY Stony Brook	72,686	54	Tennessee, Memphis	54,918
19	Case Western Reserve	72,471	55	Washington U.–St. Louis	54,675
20	Johns Hopkins	71,073	56	Rochester	54,326
21	Montreal	70,533	57	Florida State	53,883
22	Miami	70,529	58	Louisville	53,374
23	Southern California	70,072	59	Boston University	52,750
24	Vanderbilt	69,738	60	Cincinnati	51,440
25	George Washington	67,985	61	Missouri	50,533
26	Northwestern	67,825	62	Tulane	50,184
27	Dartmouth	66,595	63	Oklahoma State	49,500
28	Southern Illinois	66,247	64	Florida	48,746
29	Howard	66,000	65	Kansas	47,500
30	North Carolina	65,860	66	South Carolina	46,692
31	SUNY Buffalo	65,833	67	Texas Tech	45,634
32	Virginia	65,600		Alabama	*
33	Ohio State	65,149		Hawaii	*
34	California, Davis	64,560		Louisiana State	*
35	New York University	64,000		Tennessee, Knoxville	*
36	Georgetown	63,456		Wayne State	*

Salaries of directors are not included in the calculation of medians.
Alabama, Hawaii, Louisiana State, Tennessee–Knoxville, and Wayne State are not ranked because they reported four or fewer individuals.
Canadian salaries are expressed in US dollars.

Table 38: Average Professional Salaries in ARL University Medical Libraries Rank Order Table, FY 2011–2012

Rank	Institution	Salary	Rank	Institution	Salary
1	Toronto	98,963	37	Utah	64,626
2	Alberta	95,367	38	Arizona	64,591
3	Queen's	90,715	39	Emory	64,211
4	British Columbia	85,576	40	Dartmouth	63,819
5	Ottawa	85,060	41	Michigan	63,455
6	Harvard	83,012	42	Washington U.–St. Louis	63,365
7	Cornell	80,939	43	Minnesota	63,278
8	Calgary	80,754	44	Oklahoma	63,050
9	Connecticut	79,605	45	Southern Illinois	63,036
10	Manitoba	79,413	46	Georgetown	62,958
11	Saskatchewan	79,311	47	Illinois, Chicago	62,734
12	Yale	78,346	48	Pennsylvania State	62,662
13	California, Los Angeles	78,309	49	Pittsburgh	62,134
14	McGill	77,530	50	California, Davis	61,875
15	McMaster	75,773	51	Wisconsin	60,472
16	Montreal	75,236	52	Cincinnati	59,994
17	Southern California	74,170	53	Duke	59,946
18	Miami	74,087	54	Temple	59,147
19	SUNY Stony Brook	73,018	55	Rochester	58,325
20	Johns Hopkins	71,580	56	Louisville	57,677
21	Columbia	70,645	57	Kentucky	57,661
22	California, San Diego	70,200	58	Boston University	57,155
23	New York University	70,081	59	Florida	55,320
24	Howard	69,500	60	Tulane	54,850
25	North Carolina	69,174	61	Tennessee, Memphis	54,145
26	SUNY Buffalo	68,934	62	Oklahoma State	53,968
27	Case Western Reserve	68,651	63	Missouri	53,740
28	George Washington	68,038	64	Florida State	52,637
29	Iowa	67,896	65	Kansas	51,616
30	Ohio State	67,779	66	Texas Tech	49,315
31	Northwestern	67,350	67	South Carolina	49,291
32	Vanderbilt	66,991		Alabama	*
33	Virginia	65,786		Hawaii	*
34	Nebraska	65,518		Louisiana State	*
35	Pennsylvania	65,042		Tennessee, Knoxville	*
36	Washington	64,655		Wayne State	*

Salaries of directors are not included in the calculation of medians.
Alabama, Hawaii, Louisiana State, Tennessee–Knoxville, and Wayne State are not ranked because they reported four or fewer individuals.
Canadian salaries are expressed in US dollars.

TABLE 39: NUMBER AND AVERAGE SALARIES OF ARL UNIVERSITY MEDICAL LIBRARIANS BY POSITION AND SEX, FY 2011–2012

Position	WOMEN Salary	No.	MEN Salary	No.	TOTAL Salary	No.
Head, Medical	$130,029	52	$142,460	14	$132,666	66
Associate Director	88,803	38	96,791	14	90,953	52
Assistant Director	69,469	35	78,863	7	71,035	42
Head, Branch	‡	18	‡	1	68,970	19
Functional Specialist	67,027	70	68,139	87	67,643	157
Subject Specialist	64,686	59	68,745	10	65,274	69
Dept. Head:						
Acquisitions	67,396	15	62,445	5	66,158	20
Reference	71,127	18	85,180	5	74,182	23
Cataloging	‡	8	‡	2	67,630	10
Serials	‡	5	‡	2	60,610	7
Documents/Maps						
Circulation	64,472	9	63,380	9	63,926	18
Rare Books/Manuscripts	‡	3	‡	3	78,301	6
Computer Systems	81,100	5	87,673	7	84,934	12
Other	71,013	49	80,938	12	72,966	61
Reference:						
Over 14 years experience	71,529	94	70,966	24	71,415	118
10 to 14 years experience	67,329	39	74,173	7	68,370	46
5 to 9 years experience	58,803	41	57,228	13	58,424	54
Under 5 years experience	53,728	39	49,489	10	52,863	49
Cataloging:						
Over 14 years experience	‡	4	‡	2	62,192	6
10 to 14 years experience	54,468	4	.		54,468	4
5 to 9 years experience	47,737	4	.		47,737	4
Under 5 years experience	‡	3	.		‡	3
Other:						
Over 14 years experience	65,095	26	68,098	10	65,929	36
10 to 14 years experience	58,661	10	56,355	5	57,893	15
5 to 9 years experience	‡	14	‡	3	54,743	17
Under 5 years experience	‡	13	‡	3	58,073	16
All Positions	**$72,001**	**675**	**$74,082**	**255**	**$72,571**	**930**

Canadian salaries are expressed in US dollars.

‡ Salary data are not published when fewer than four individuals are involved in either category.

. No positions reported in this category.

TABLE 40: Number and Average Years of Experience of ARL University Medical Librarians by Position And Sex, FY 2011–2012

Position	WOMEN		MEN		TOTAL	
	Years	No.	Years	No.	Years	No.
Head, Medical	29.7	52	32.1	14	30.2	66
Associate Director	24.7	38	27.8	14	25.5	52
Assistant Director	22.6	35	13.9	7	21.2	42
Head, Branch	18.9	18	8.0	1	18.4	19
Functional Specialist	13.4	70	11.6	87	12.4	157
Subject Specialist	13.6	59	12.8	10	13.5	69
Dept. Head:						
Acquisitions	21.3	15	17.6	5	20.4	20
Reference	22.9	18	20.6	5	22.4	23
Cataloging	19.4	8	23.5	2	20.2	10
Serials	19.6	5	16.5	2	18.7	7
Documents/Maps	.		.		.	
Circulation	21.4	9	11.4	9	16.4	18
Rare Books/Manuscripts	23.0	3	26.3	3	24.7	6
Computer Systems	18.2	5	18.7	7	18.5	12
Other	19.0	49	19.2	12	19.1	61
Public services	12.9	39	15.0	8	13.3	47
Technical services	19.8	9	16.0	7	18.1	16
Administration	14.6	15	16.5	6	15.1	21
Reference	15.4	213	14.1	54	15.1	267
Cataloger	10.7	15	35.5	2	13.6	17
All Positions	**17.7**	**675**	**15.9**	**255**	**17.2**	**930**

. No positions were reported in this category.

Table 41: Number and Average Salaries of ARL University Medical Librarians by Years of Experience and Sex, FY 2011–2012

Experience	WOMEN Salary	No.	MEN Salary	No.	TOTAL Salary	No.	% OF TOTAL
0–3 years	$56,962	75	$67,162	30	$59,876	105	11%
4–7 years	58,083	96	61,312	50	59,189	146	16%
8–11 years	64,199	84	70,174	30	65,771	114	12%
12–15 years	68,454	75	70,455	29	69,012	104	11%
16–19 years	75,044	57	70,668	29	73,569	86	9%
20–23 years	70,738	64	80,677	19	73,013	83	9%
24–27 years	78,424	57	90,277	14	80,761	71	8%
28–31 years	85,642	54	88,309	19	86,336	73	8%
32–35 years	88,655	56	81,209	23	86,487	79	8%
over 35 years	94,058	57	105,853	12	96,110	69	7%
All Positions	**$72,001**	**675**	**$74,082**	**255**	**$72,571**	**930**	**100%**

Canadian salaries are expressed in US dollars.

ARL University Law Libraries

Tables 42–48

TABLE 42: FILLED POSITIONS; AVERAGE, MEDIAN, AND BEGINNING SALARIES; AND AVERAGE YEARS OF EXPERIENCE IN ARL UNIVERSITY LAW LIBRARIES, FY 2011–2012

Institution	Filled Positions	Average Salary	Median Salary	Beginning Salary	Average Yrs. Exp.
Alberta	3	‡	‡	56,667	28.3
Arizona	9	64,734	62,671	55,000	17.2
Arizona State	6	67,330	70,000	50,000	24.8
Boston	12	75,309	72,300	55,000	17.4
Boston College	15	72,433	68,330	44,050	17.2
British Columbia	3	‡	‡	55,258	24.7
Calgary	2	‡	‡	57,919	14.5
California, Davis	7	76,418	72,300	46,164	20.6
California, Irvine	6	88,973	82,524	46,164	12.5
California, Los Angeles	16	80,883	87,887	46,164	15.9
Case Western Reserve	12	70,456	69,500	35,700	21.3
Cincinnati	8	67,567	62,340	50,000	17.8
Colorado	7	68,285	58,603	45,000	18.1
Columbia	17	80,863	73,298	60,000	14.6
Connecticut	8	78,303	77,706	41,875	20.9
Cornell	8	81,310	75,013	61,000	15.6
Duke	11	71,485	64,450	61,000	15.6
Emory	11	60,653	58,766	42,000	12.0
Florida	8	58,379	53,162	50,000	12.8
Florida State	9	56,168	54,329	50,000	20.0
George Washington	21	93,002	85,983	50,000	17.2
Georgetown	27	85,347	78,415	54,000	13.6
Georgia	8	56,448	55,752	57,500	12.0
Harvard	48	81,990	77,472	59,691	13.8
Hawaii	6	85,440	82,392	57,504	13.7
Houston	13	56,004	52,676	58,000	16.8
Howard	8	54,479	53,520	51,000	22.5
Illinois, Urbana	10	63,325	64,129	53,500	16.0
Indiana	9	72,526	68,533	40,400	21.4
Iowa	15	76,977	76,075	43,000	22.1
Kansas	6	52,143	52,555	41,500	9.2
Kentucky	7	55,073	52,775	50,000	11.4
Louisiana State	9	57,380	55,846	42,500	18.8
Louisville	6	61,855	61,729	38,000	21.3
McGill	4	‡	‡	49,930	16.8
Manitoba	3	‡	‡	49,743	30.3
Miami	12	59,491	59,876	45,000	17.7
Michigan	9	86,620	87,927	49,000	18.7
Minnesota	13	79,779	77,673	44,000	19.8
Missouri	8	55,073	57,327	40,000	14.6
Montreal	4	‡	‡	54,076	13.8
Nebraska	6	65,180	60,393	45,000	16.7

TABLE 42: FILLED POSITIONS; AVERAGE, MEDIAN, AND BEGINNING SALARIES; AND AVERAGE YEARS OF EXPERIENCE IN ARL UNIVERSITY LAW LIBRARIES, FY 2011–2012

Institution	Filled Positions	Average Salary	Median Salary	Beginning Salary	Average Yrs. Exp.
New Mexico	8	69,996	69,760	50,000	13.6
New York	19	81,352	77,686	60,000	23.6
North Carolina	12	68,735	65,268	57,000	16.2
Northwestern	10	64,948	60,598	50,000	22.8
Notre Dame	14	72,110	67,825	44,000	19.1
Ohio State	7	67,788	59,993	46,000	11.7
Oklahoma	7	59,551	52,852	42,000	16.9
Oregon	7	57,483	55,923	42,000	16.4
Ottawa	3	‡	‡	50,111	23.7
Pennsylvania	14	69,684	67,800	45,000	17.3
Pennsylvania State	9	71,808	69,586	57,000	21.7
Queen's	3	‡	‡	53,842	11.7
Rutgers – Newark	6	69,919	79,773	62,000	19.2
Rutgers – Camden	8	80,884	68,983	67,500	22.1
Saskatchewan	2	‡	‡	57,839	19.0
South Carolina	8	66,342	67,750	50,000	18.8
Southern Illinois	4	‡	‡	50,000	8.0
Suny–Buffalo	10	72,770	72,791	55,000	16.3
Syracuse	10	58,823	55,631	46,700	15.4
Temple	10	63,848	53,203	43,500	25.1
Tennessee	8	58,966	55,998	45,000	12.0
Texas	14	67,223	57,057	42,000	16.1
Texas Tech	8	60,073	56,312	50,000	10.0
Toronto	6	90,595	95,584	54,524	13.8
Tulane	8	62,911	60,940	45,000	17.1
Utah	8	56,402	52,530	41,500	18.5
Vanderbilt	5	69,663	61,994	41,500	18.8
Virginia	13	70,592	64,650	63,500	16.9
Washington	16	71,318	65,496	61,000	22.5
Washington U.–St. Louis	10	65,037	60,409	50,000	20.9
Wayne State	5	61,830	57,360	45,600	20.2
Western Ontario	3	‡	‡	53,925	16.3
Wisconsin	12	67,501	63,725	40,526	25.1
Yale	20	85,636	78,000	49,500	17.0
York	5	97,812	101,244	48,931	17.2

Directors are included in figures for filled positions and average years of experience, but not in either the average or median salary statistics. Canadian salaries are expressed in US dollars.

‡ Salary data are not published when fewer than four individuals are involved.

TABLE 43: BEGINNING PROFESSIONAL SALARIES IN ARL UNIVERSITY LAW LIBRARIES RANK ORDER TABLE, FY 2011–2012

Rank	Institution	Salary	Rank	Institution	Salary
1	Rutgers, Newark	67,500	30	Texas Tech	50,000
2	Virginia	63,500	30	Washington U.–St. Louis	50,000
3	Rutgers, Camden	62,000	42	McGill	49,930
4	Cornell	61,000	43	Manitoba	49,743
4	Duke	61,000	44	Yale	49,500
4	Washington	61,000	45	Michigan	49,000
7	Columbia	60,000	46	York	48,931
7	New York University	60,000	47	Syracuse	46,700
9	Harvard	59,691	48	California, Davis	46,164
10	Houston	58,000	48	California, Irvine	46,164
11	Calgary	57,919	48	California, Los Angeles	46,164
12	Saskatchewan	57,839	51	Ohio State	46,000
13	Hawaii	57,504	52	Wayne State	45,600
14	Georgia	57,500	53	Colorado	45,000
15	North Carolina	57,000	53	Miami	45,000
15	Pennsylvania State	57,000	53	Nebraska	45,000
17	Alberta	56,667	53	Pennsylvania	45,000
18	British Columbia	55,258	53	Tennessee	45,000
19	Arizona	55,000	53	Tulane	45,000
19	Boston University	55,000	59	Boston College	44,050
19	SUNY Buffalo	55,000	60	Minnesota	44,000
22	Toronto	54,524	60	Notre Dame	44,000
23	Montreal	54,076	62	Temple	43,500
24	Georgetown	54,000	63	Iowa	43,000
25	Western Ontario	53,925	64	Louisiana State	42,500
26	Queen's	53,842	65	Emory	42,000
27	Illinois, Urbana	53,500	65	Oklahoma	42,000
28	Howard	51,000	65	Oregon	42,000
29	Ottawa	50,111	65	Texas	42,000
30	Arizona State	50,000	69	Connecticut	41,875
30	Cincinnati	50,000	70	Kansas	41,500
30	Florida	50,000	70	Utah	41,500
30	Florida State	50,000	70	Vanderbilt	41,500
30	George Washington	50,000	73	Wisconsin	40,526
30	Kentucky	50,000	74	Indiana	40,400
30	New Mexico	50,000	75	Missouri	40,000
30	Northwestern	50,000	76	Louisville	38,000
30	South Carolina	50,000	77	Case Western Reserve	35,700
30	Southern Illinois	50,000			

Beginning salary figures represent officially designated base, not necessarily salaries of actual incumbents.
Canadian salaries are expressed in US dollars.

Table 44: Median Professional Salaries in ARL University Law Libraries

Rank Order Table, FY 2011–2012

Rank	Institution	Salary	Rank	Institution	Salary
1	York	101,244	40	Louisville	61,729
2	Toronto	95,584	41	Tulane	60,940
3	Michigan	87,927	42	Northwestern	60,598
4	California, Los Angeles	87,887	43	Washington U.–St. Louis	60,409
5	George Washington	85,983	44	Nebraska	60,393
6	California, Irvine	82,524	45	Ohio State	59,993
7	Hawaii	82,392	46	Miami	59,876
8	Rutgers, Camden	79,773	47	Emory	58,766
9	Georgetown	78,415	48	Colorado	58,603
10	Yale	78,000	49	Wayne State	57,360
11	Connecticut	77,706	50	Missouri	57,327
12	New York University	77,686	51	Texas	57,057
13	Minnesota	77,673	52	Texas Tech	56,312
14	Harvard	77,472	53	Tennessee	55,998
15	Iowa	76,075	54	Oregon	55,923
16	Cornell	75,013	55	Louisiana State	55,846
17	Columbia	73,298	56	Georgia	55,752
18	SUNY Buffalo	72,791	57	Syracuse	55,631
19	Boston University	72,300	58	Florida State	54,329
19	California, Davis	72,300	59	Howard	53,520
21	Arizona State	70,000	60	Temple	53,203
22	New Mexico	69,760	61	Florida	53,162
23	Pennsylvania State	69,586	62	Oklahoma	52,852
24	Case Western Reserve	69,500	63	Kentucky	52,775
25	Rutgers, Newark	68,983	64	Houston	52,676
26	Indiana	68,533	65	Kansas	52,555
27	Boston College	68,330	66	Utah	52,530
28	Notre Dame	67,825		Alberta	*
29	Pennsylvania	67,800		British Columbia	*
30	South Carolina	67,750		Calgary	*
31	Washington	65,496		McGill	*
32	North Carolina	65,268		Manitoba	*
33	Virginia	64,650		Montreal	*
34	Duke	64,450		Ottawa	*
35	Illinois, Urbana	64,129		Queen's	*
36	Wisconsin	63,725		Saskatchewan	*
37	Arizona	62,671		Southern Illinois	*
38	Cincinnati	62,340		Western Ontario	*
39	Vanderbilt	61,994			

Salaries of directors are not included in the calculation of medians.

Alberta, British Columbia, Calgary, McGill, Manitoba, Montreal, Ottawa, Queen's, Saskatchewan, Southern Illinois, and Western Ontario are not ranked because they reported four or fewer individuals.

Canadian salaries are expressed in US dollars.

Table 45: Average Professional Salaries in ARL University Law Libraries
Rank Order Table, FY 2011–2012

Rank	Institution	Salary	Rank	Institution	Salary
1	York	97,812	40	South Carolina	66,342
2	George Washington	93,002	41	Nebraska	65,180
3	Toronto	90,595	42	Washington U.–St. Louis	65,037
4	California, Irvine	88,973	43	Northwestern	64,948
5	Michigan	86,620	44	Arizona	64,734
6	Yale	85,636	45	Temple	63,848
7	Hawaii	85,440	46	Illinois, Urbana	63,325
8	Georgetown	85,347	47	Tulane	62,911
9	Harvard	81,990	48	Louisville	61,855
10	New York University	81,352	49	Wayne State	61,830
11	Cornell	81,310	50	Emory	60,653
12	Rutgers, Newark	80,884	51	Texas Tech	60,073
13	California, Los Angeles	80,883	52	Oklahoma	59,551
14	Columbia	80,863	53	Miami	59,491
15	Minnesota	79,779	54	Tennessee	58,966
16	Connecticut	78,303	55	Syracuse	58,823
17	Iowa	76,977	56	Florida	58,379
18	California, Davis	76,418	57	Oregon	57,483
19	Boston University	75,309	58	Louisiana State	57,380
20	SUNY Buffalo	72,770	59	Georgia	56,448
21	Indiana	72,526	60	Utah	56,402
22	Boston College	72,433	61	Florida State	56,168
23	Notre Dame	72,110	62	Houston	56,004
24	Pennsylvania State	71,808	63	Missouri	55,073
25	Duke	71,485	64	Kentucky	55,073
26	Washington	71,318	65	Howard	54,479
27	Virginia	70,592	66	Kansas	52,143
28	Case Western Reserve	70,456		Alberta	*
29	New Mexico	69,996		British Columbia	*
30	Rutgers, Camden	69,919		Calgary	*
31	Pennsylvania	69,684		McGill	*
32	Vanderbilt	69,663		Manitoba	*
33	North Carolina	68,735		Montreal	*
34	Colorado	68,285		Ottawa	*
35	Ohio State	67,788		Queen's	*
36	Cincinnati	67,567		Saskatchewan	*
37	Wisconsin	67,501		Southern Illinois	*
38	Arizona State	67,330		Western Ontario	*
39	Texas	67,223			

Salaries of directors are not included in the calculation of medians.

Alberta, British Columbia, Calgary, McGill, Manitoba, Montreal, Ottawa, Queen's, Saskatchewan, Southern Illinois, and Western Ontario are not ranked because they reported four or fewer individuals.

Canadian salaries are expressed in US dollars.

TABLE 46: NUMBER AND AVERAGE SALARIES OF ARL UNIVERSITY LAW LIBRARIANS BY POSITION AND SEX, FY 2011–2012

Position	WOMEN Salary	No.	MEN Salary	No.	TOTAL Salary	No.
Head, Law	$156,685	42	$158,353	33	$157,419	75
Associate Director	103,486	33	100,866	19	102,529	52
Assistant Director	87,633	32	88,578	16	87,948	48
Functional Specialist	61,724	22	72,589	32	68,163	54
Subject Specialist	67,729	21	71,960	7	68,787	28
Dept. Head:						
Acquisitions	68,204	27	69,573	9	68,546	36
Reference	79,851	17	76,602	7	78,903	24
Cataloging	71,165	23	71,188	5	71,169	28
Serials	‡	6	‡	1	75,156	7
Documents/Maps	‡	7	‡	2	68,663	9
Circulation	64,292	19	63,790	8	64,143	27
Rare Books/Manuscripts	92,273	4	.		92,273	4
Computer Systems	‡	2	‡	4	76,034	6
Other	75,119	17	69,440	11	72,888	28
Reference:						
Over 14 years experience	77,141	48	75,899	23	76,739	71
10 to 14 years experience	65,580	16	63,817	11	64,862	27
5 to 9 years experience	65,031	35	64,378	25	64,759	60
Under 5 years experience	62,844	45	59,933	23	61,859	68
Cataloging:						
Over 14 years experience	65,652	22	75,508	6	67,764	28
10 to 14 years experience	‡	4	‡	1	62,053	5
5 to 9 years experience	63,232	4	.		63,232	4
Under 5 years experience	‡	3	‡	3	57,736	6
Other:						
Over 14 years experience	67,001	16	68,128	4	67,226	20
10 to 14 years experience	‡	3	‡	3	58,739	6
5 to 9 years experience	‡	5	‡	3	56,558	8
Under 5 years experience	53,843	9	52,948	4	53,567	13
All Positions	**$79,452**	**482**	**$83,503**	**260**	**$80,872**	**742**

Canadian salaries are expressed in US dollars.

‡ Salary data are not published when fewer than four individuals are involved in either category.

. No positions were reported in this category.

TABLE 47: NUMBER AND AVERAGE YEARS OF EXPERIENCE OF ARL UNIVERSITY LAW LIBRARIANS BY POSITION AND SEX, FY 2011–2012

Position	WOMEN		MEN		TOTAL	
	Years	No.	Years	No.	Years	No.
Head, Law	28.8	42	25.3	33	27.3	75
Associate Director	23.1	33	21.3	19	22.4	52
Assistant Director	22.7	32	20.4	16	21.9	48
Functional Specialist	11.1	22	12.3	32	11.8	54
Subject Specialist	17.6	21	18.0	7	17.7	28
Dept. Head:						
Acquisitions	22.3	27	16.3	9	20.8	36
Reference	16.2	17	19.4	7	17.2	24
Cataloging	26.8	23	20.6	5	25.7	28
Serials	23.7	6	9.0	1	21.6	7
Documents/Maps	29.3	7	9.5	2	24.9	9
Circulation	17.1	19	12.5	8	15.7	27
Rare Books/Manuscripts	13.8	4	.		13.8	4
Computer Systems	23.5	2	13.5	4	16.8	6
Other	20.2	17	15.7	11	18.5	28
Public services	13.7	9	13.9	7	13.8	16
Technical services	16.1	14	8.7	6	13.9	20
Administration	16.4	10	26.0	1	17.3	11
Reference	12.2	144	11.2	82	11.9	226
Cataloger	19.7	33	18.8	10	19.5	43
All Positions	**18.3**	**482**	**15.8**	**260**	**17.5**	**742**

. No positions were reported in this category.

TABLE 48: NUMBER AND AVERAGE SALARIES OF ARL UNIVERSITY LAW LIBRARIANS BY YEARS OF EXPERIENCE AND SEX, FY 2011–2012

Experience	WOMEN		MEN		TOTAL		% OF TOTAL
	Salary	No.	Salary	No.	Salary	No.	
0–3 years	$60,349	53	$62,319	34	$61,119	87	12%
4–7 years	65,660	68	63,004	49	64,548	117	16%
8–11 years	70,099	52	72,864	30	71,111	82	11%
12–15 years	72,490	52	78,880	26	74,620	78	11%
16–19 years	76,074	50	93,087	22	81,272	72	10%
20–23 years	86,448	44	93,321	25	88,938	69	9%
24–27 years	88,028	30	84,890	28	86,513	58	8%
28–31 years	91,842	42	120,673	19	100,822	61	8%
32–35 years	96,331	40	119,507	18	103,524	58	8%
over 35 years	103,120	51	118,476	9	105,423	60	8%
All Positions	**$79,452**	**482**	**$83,503**	**260**	**$80,872**	**742**	**100%**

Canadian salaries are expressed in US dollars.

‡ Salary data are not published when fewer than four individuals are involved in either category.

University Library Questionnaire and Instructions

ASSOCIATION OF RESEARCH LIBRARIES

ARL ANNUAL SALARY SURVEY 2011-12
University Library Questionnaire
GENERAL AND DATA INPUT (EXCEL) INSTRUCTIONS

http://www.arl.org/stats/annualsurveys/salary/

GENERAL OVERVIEW

- **Use the newly available Web form for your data submission:**
  University Libraries: http://www.formstack.com/forms/?1093982-c6BynijupA
  Fill in Part I on the Web and upload your file for Part II through the same interface.
  NOTE: You must complete the entire submission in a single session. The Web interface
  does **NOT** allow you to return and edit your information once it is submitted.

- **This survey is concerned with professional positions only.** Since the criteria for
  determining professional status vary among libraries, there is no attempt to define the term
  "professional." Each library should report the salaries of those staff members it considers
  professionals, irrespective of faculty status or membership in a collective bargaining unit,
  including, when appropriate, staff who are not librarians in the strict sense of the term, such
  as computer experts, systems analysts, budget officers, etc.

- **Report individual salaries for the Main, Law, and Medical library on the separate
  template using Microsoft Excel (see
  http://www.arl.org/stats/annualsurveys/salary/salform11.shtml).** A generic template is
  available. Add your institution's ARL Library Institution Code [LibID]. (See
  http://www.arl.org/stats/annualsurveys/surveycoord/instno_inam.shtml if you do not
  know your code.)

- **Use "Percent" to determine if an employee works full-time or part-time.** All full-time
  employees have Percent = 1.00, i.e., they work 100% of a full-time schedule. If Percent is less
  than 1.00, then the employee works that fraction of a full-time schedule. For example, a 65%
  time appointment would be entered as 0.65. Calculate the percent appointment by dividing
  the amount of time an employee works by the amount considered to be the norm for full-
  time employment at your institution. For example, if a full-time appointment at your
  institution is 12 months at 40 hours per week:
  - A 9-month part-time appointment has Percent = 9/12, or 0.75.
  - An appointment at 30 hours per week has Percent = 30/40, also 0.75.
  - An appointment at 30 hours and 9 months has Percent = 0.75 x 0.75 = 0.56.

21 Dupont Circle NW, Suite 800
Washington, DC 20036

202 296 2296 telephone
202 872 0884 fax
http://www.arl.org

Enter Percent with two decimal points.

- **Report salaries for both full-time and part-time professional positions**. Salaries for part-time positions should **NOT** be converted to their full-time equivalents. Report the actual part-time salary paid and indicate the percent appointment for that employee in the appropriate column.

- **Include salaries for all professional positions, regardless of whether the salaries come from regular library budget funds <u>or from special funds such as research grants</u>**. Please include all professionals involved in the provision of library services, including **contract-supported positions**.

- **The salary figures should be straight gross salary figures. <u>Do not include fringe benefits</u>.**

- **Provide explanatory footnotes to the reported figures, when necessary, at the end of Part I.** Footnotes will be included in the published survey, where appropriate.

- **After all data have been entered, make a backup copy of the complete file for your institution's master file**. Your backup should include individual names/ID numbers. NOTE: The data submitted to ARL should NOT include individual names/ID numbers, so <u>ARL will NOT be able to supply a copy of your institution's complete file next year</u>.

- **Please return the questionnaire the ARL Statistics and Assessment Program by <u>October 1, 2011.</u> Be sure to keep a complete copy of your return, including the electronic version of the data for your files**.

INSTRUCTIONS

Part I: Summary Data (Microsoft Word Form)

1. Part I of this survey deals with general information for the current fiscal year, 2011-12.

2. Include the Beginning Professional Salary for Law and Medical libraries if included in the survey.

3. The Beginning Professional Salary is the salary that **would** be paid to a **newly hired professional without experience**, not necessarily the lowest professional salary paid. In reporting the beginning salary, please use a figure that is actually used or likely to be used for entry-level librarians hired by your library, even if it is your practice rarely to hire entry-level professionals without experience.

4. Please report the **2011-12** Beginning Professional Salary <u>to the best of your knowledge</u> as it exists on July 1, 2011. Do not delay returning your survey with the expectation that more information will be available later.

5. The 2011-12 Average and Median Salary figures will be calculated by ARL from the individual data supplied.

6. Be sure to fill in the name of the reporting library and the name of the person who prepares the report.

Part II: Individual Data (Microsoft Excel Form)

1. Part II of this survey requests information on salary, sex, minority status, rank, and years of experience for all filled positions for fiscal year 2011-12. The survey requests information for individuals; aggregate data for each institution will be generated by computer. Vacant positions should be excluded from your report.

2. Data for the Main, Law, and Medical libraries should be reported on separate Excel files.

3. **Obtain the Excel file.** These instructions assume that you have Microsoft Excel available for use. If not, or if you have trouble opening the files in Excel, please call the ARL Statistics and Assessment Program at (202) 296-2296 or email stats@arl.org.

4. The template Excel file is available at:
http://www.arl.org/stats/annualsurveys/salary/salform11.shtml. This is a generic, blank file that can hold data for Main, Law, or Medical libraries. The file's name is "sal11xxxx.xls"; open the file and save it to your own computer by choosing "Save As" under the File menu. When saving the file, utilize ARL as the prefix for main library reports, use 11 to designate the year (2011-12), and change the "xxxx" in its name to your ARL institution code number, e.g., "ARL111150.xls." Note: use MED for medical libraries, e.g. "MED111150" and LAW to denote law libraries, e.g., "LAW111150."

> The file contains columns labeled as follows:
> Required: Name/ID# LibID Page Line Salary Job Sex OEOcat Yrsexp Rank Percent
> Optional: Hisp NatAm Asian Black HawPI White

In the LibID column, enter your ARL Library Institution Code. (See http://www.arl.org/stats/annualsurveys/surveycoord/instno_inam.shtml if you do not know your code.) If you leave this column blank we will fill it in for you when we receive the data.

Columns labeled "Page," "Line," and "Percent" are already filled for you. The numbers in the "Page" and "Line" columns will be used to identify these positions in case of data errors; do not change them. Eleven "pages" of 25 lines each have been provided; if this is not sufficient to list all positions at your institution, copy and paste lines 1-25 of the last page as needed.

Entering Data for Part II: Individual Data (Microsoft Excel Form)

1. The "Name/ID#" column is for your internal use, to enter and verify information for staff members by name. ARL does not require that you submit the information in this field to ARL. Please delete this column before sending the file to ARL. Upon receiving this file, ARL will delete any data in this column if you have not deleted them already.

2. The "LibID" will hold your institution's ARL number, for identification purposes. If you do not know your ARL number, you can find it on the Web under ARL Library Institution Codes. If you leave this column blank, it will be filled in by ARL staff.

3. "Salary" should be entered as it existed on July 1, 2011. Please do not hold up the reporting process for later salary adjustments. Include all filled positions and exclude all vacant positions. Report the actual salary paid. Do not adjust part-time salaries to their full-time equivalents; ARL will do this during the data analysis and verification stage. Do not include fringe benefits.

4. Each position can have only one "Job" code, to be taken from the following list:

DIRLIB Director of Libraries (includes Dean of Libraries and equivalent titles)
ASCDIR Associate Director
ASTDIR Assistant Director
HDMED Head, Medical Library (Human Medicine only)
HDLAW Head, Law Library
HDBR Head, Other Branch Library (including Veterinary Medicine)
FSPEC Functional Specialist
  ARCH Archivists/Curators
  BUSI Budget/Fiscal/Business Manager/Facilities
  HUMRES Human Resources/Training/Staff Development
  ITS Information Technology Systems
  ITW Information Technology Web Development
  ITP Information Technology Programming/Application Development
  MEDIA Media/Multimedia Specialists (including graphics)
  PRES Preservation/Conservation
SSPEC Subject Specialist
HDACQ Head, Acquisitions Department
HDCAT Head, Catalog Department/Unit
HDCIRC Head, Circulation
HDCOMP Head, Library and Computer Systems
HDDOC Head, Documents Department
HDMAP Head, Map Room/Department
HDRBM Head, Rare Book/Manuscripts Department
HDREF Head, Reference Department
HDSER Head, Serials Department
HDOTH Head, Other Department/Service/Agency
CAT Catalogers, both general and specialized
REF Reference librarians, both general and specialized
PUBS Public Services, non-supervisory, except reference librarians
TECH Technical Services, non-supervisory, except catalogers
ADMIN Administrative and other units, non-supervisory position

The position categories used in this survey are intended to correspond roughly with the activities carried on in libraries, not with any particular pattern of staff organization or nomenclature. Please use these categories in the manner you feel best applies to your library. If any individual has responsibilities described by more than one of the above categories, choose the category that is most typical of his/her general duties.

Associate or Assistant Director, and Head, Other Branch. Use these codes for all persons at these levels regardless of the area of specialty. If an assistant or associate director is also head of a department, choose the category that most reflects the general duties of the person currently in the position.

Specialists. These are of two kinds: Subject Specialists primarily build collections, but may also offer specialized reference and bibliographic services; Functional Specialists are media specialists or experts in management fields such as personnel, fiscal matters, systems, preservation, etc. Specialists may not be, strictly speaking, professional librarians (i.e., have an MLS). The "specialist" category would generally not be used for someone with significant supervisory responsibilities, who should instead be listed as a department head or assistant director (see also note under Assistant Department Head, below).

Functional Specialist sub-codes. Starting with the 2004-05 Salary Survey, the ARL Statistics and Assessment Committee adopted a proposal from the ACRL Personnel Administrators and Staff Development Officers Discussion Group to break down the Functional Specialist category. For each position which would have been labeled FSPEC prior to 2004-05, instead please use one of the eight sub-codes (ARCH, BUSI, HUMRES, ITS, ITW, ITP, MEDIA, PRES) to describe that position. If you cannot determine which sub-code to use, please use the FSPEC code.

Department Heads. Department Heads not specifically included in the above list should be included under the category "Head, Other Department/Service/Agency." Head, Catalog Department should be used either for the department that handles all cataloging, or for the head of a specialized cataloging unit (e.g. copy cataloging or foreign languages). List the head of library automation and computer systems, applications, programming, etc. as HDCOMP unless that person is also an Associate or Assistant Director, in which case use the appropriate administrative code. If there is an intermediate level of management between an Associate or Assistant Director and the professionals who actually carry out the analysis, programming, etc., use HDCOMP to define that intermediate level. Professionals who carry out analysis, programming, etc., should be listed as functional specialists (FSPEC).

Head, Acquisitions Department. Use HDACQ for all of the following positions: (a) head of a department that is responsible for the selection of material (or management of selection activities carried out on a basis encompassing more than a single organizational unit), but not responsible for the placement of orders, payment of invoices, etc.; (b) head of a department responsible for the placement of orders, maintaining on-order files, payment of invoices, etc., but not responsible for selection decisions; (c) head of a department responsible for both the selection decisions (or coordination of selection activities) and for acquiring the material. Libraries that split these two functions between two departments should report more than one professional with the position HDACQ.

Special note concerning Assistant Department Heads. Assistant Department Heads who are responsible for major units and spend the bulk of their time in supervision and revision of the work of others should also be listed as "Head, Other Department/Service/Agency." See additional subcodes below for Head, Cataloging, and Head, Other Department. However, Assistant Head positions responsible for small units or for supervision only in the absence of the head should be reported as non-supervisory or specialist positions as appropriate.]

Administrative. Please note that ADMIN is not only for Administrative Services and related positions, but also can be applied to Public Relations/Communications,

Development/Fundraising, and all other administrative and/or professional positions which do not have a logical home elsewhere.

5. **Please indicate "Sex" with the letter M or F**, indicating male or female, respectively.

6. **"OEOCat" minority status code**, for U.S. university libraries only, should be indicated with one of the following code numbers. (Leave blank if a Canadian library):

   1 = Black
   2 = Hispanic
   3 = Asian or Pacific Islander
   4 = American Indian or Native Alaskan
   5 = Caucasian/Other

7. **"YrsExp," or total years of professional experience.** For most professional staff members this will mean counting the years since the MLS degree was awarded. When counting, do not subtract interim periods when an individual was not engaged in professional library employment if these periods are short in relation to the overall professional career. Count an academic year contract period as a full year. Be sure to include professional experience in previous positions and in other institutions. The figure should be rounded off to the nearest whole number; for example, a position with 14.5 years of experience would appear as 15.

8. **Indicate "Rank" using the following system of codes**:

   0   The library director. Some systems also use 0 for assistant and/or associate directors.
   1   Lowest level in the rank structure, such as an entry-level position.
   2-8 Successively higher levels; for example, 5 indicates a higher rank than 2.
   9   Rank cannot be determined, or, the individual is outside the organization's rank structure.

NOTE: These codes are meant to be *guides only*. Do not recode your rank system into an 8 level system if your rank system does not have eight levels. Please code each employee with his or her *actual* rank at your institution. When coding the library director as "0", do not add or subtract a level to or from your ranking system.

Responses concerning rank should be limited to professional librarians, and other professionals who occupy the same ranks as librarians. **Leave the rank column blank for professionals who do not occupy these ranks or if the column is not applicable.** For example, if the Library Business Officer holds a rank typically used for university administrators but not for librarians, do not supply a rank code for that individual, even if you have included salary and other data.

If multiple ranking structures are used for librarians and these structures are substantially different and not equivalent, enter individual rank information only for that group which represents the largest fraction of "rank-and-file" librarians.

The maximum number of ranks reported here must not exceed the maximum number of rank-levels reported in Part I for individual data under Rank structure. When counting the total number of rank levels, include ranks that may be unoccupied at the present time due to circumstances like unusually high turnover, hiring freezes, etc.

9. **"Percent"** is used to determine if an employee works full-time or part-time. All full-time employees have Percent = 1.00, i.e., they work 100% of a full-time schedule. If Percent is less than 1.00, then the employee works that fraction of a full-time schedule. For example, a 65% time appointment would be entered as 0.65. Calculate the percent appointment by dividing the amount of time an employee works by the amount considered to be the norm for full-time employment at your institution. For example, if a full-time appointment at your institution is 12 months at 40 hours per week:

- o A 9-month part-time appointment has Percent = 9/12, or 0.75.
- o An appointment at 30 hours per week has Percent = 30/40, also 0.75.
- o An appointment at 30 hours and 9 months has Percent = 0.75 x 0.75 = 0.56.

Enter Percent with two decimal points.

Optional Questions: (Shown on printed forms as the last six columns)

Please complete as much of this section as possible (US libraries only), but do not hold up the reporting process if some of the data requested are not available. Canadian libraries should leave these columns blank. The major change in the revised standard for the classification of federal data on race and ethnicity is that now respondents are able to report more than one race by choosing multiple responses to the following questions

Race and Ethnicity: The U.S. Office of Management and Budget has revised the Standards for the Classification of Federal Data on Race and Ethnicity and according to the new standard there will be five minimum categories for data on race (American Indian or Alaska Native, Asian, Black or African American, Native Hawaiian or Other Pacific Islander, and White) and one category for data on ethnicity ("Hispanic or Latino"). **Respondents will be able to report more than one race by choosing multiple responses to the race question.** The purpose of the revised classification is to reflect the increasing diversity of the U.S. population that has resulted primarily from growth in immigration and in interracial marriages. The new standards were used by the Bureau of the Census in the 2000 decennial census.[1] In light of these developments, we are collecting the new classification on race and ethnicity in the *ARL Annual Salary Survey on an **optional** basis.*

Ethnicity should be indicated by coding 1 to indicate if the person is of Hispanic or Latino ethnicity, and coding 0 otherwise. The definition of Hispanic or Latino ethnicity is: A person of Cuban, Mexican, Puerto Rican, Cuban, South or Central American, or other Spanish culture or origin, regardless of race.

Race should be indicated for U.S. university libraries only, by choosing one or more responses among the five racial categories provided here; 1=yes and 0=no. You can select multiple racial categories for a person. The definitions of the five racial categories, listed with their respective column names, are:

American Indian or Alaska Native (NatAm): A person having origins in any of the original peoples of North and South America (including Central America) who maintains tribal affiliation or community attachment.

---

[1] http://www.census.gov/population/www/socdemo/race/racefactcb.html

Asian (Asian): A person having origins in any of the original peoples of the Far East, Southeast Asia, or the Indian subcontinent including, for example, Cambodia, China, India, Japan, Korea, Malaysia, Pakistan, the Philippine Islands, Thailand, and Vietnam.

Black or African American (Black): A person having origins in any of the black racial groups of Africa.

Native Hawaiian or Other Pacific Islander (HawPI): A person having origins in any of the original peoples of Hawaii, Guam, Samoa, or other Pacific Islands.

White (White): A person having origins in any of the original peoples of Europe, the Middle East, or North Africa.

Submitting the Data for Part I and Part II on the Web

ARL is using the online services of FormStack to collect the data. As part of its privacy policy, FormStack pledges not to sell any collected information to third parties. For the complete FormStack privacy policy, visit http://www.formstack.com/privacy.html. ARL also accepts Part I and Part II of the salary survey by e-mail from those users who may be uncomfortable submitting the files in FormStack:

- University Libraries: http://www.formstack.com/forms/?1093982-c6BynijupA

Be sure to have the electronic copy of your completed salary survey Excel file handy as you will be submitting this file via the FormStack Web form. In addition to the completed Excel file, be prepared to provide the following information as well:

  o The name, title, email and phone number of the person who prepared the Excel file. The name, title, email and phone number of your institution's contact person for the salary survey (if different from the person who prepared the Excel file)

  o Indicate whether you are submitting salary information for one or more of the following: Main, Law, or Medical library, and the beginning professional salary and rank structure for each.

  o **For professional salary** list the salary that would be paid to a newly hired professional without experience (even if local practice discourages hiring entry-level professionals without experience). Please report the 2011-12 beginning professional salary to the best of your knowledge as it existed on July 1, 2011.

  o **For rank structure**, list the number of unique levels in your institution's rank structure. If you have no levels in your rank structure, use 1. The number reported here should be equal to the highest number in the "Rank" column of your Excel file (i.e., the number of levels reported in your Excel file should equal the number of levels reported here).

  o The names of the libraries that are included and excluded in your figures for the 'general libraries' (these can be main campus libraries or branch campus libraries), as well as any other explanatory information, should be indicated in a footnote. In your footnotes, report any information that would clarify the figures submitted: the inclusion and exclusion of branch campus libraries, a reporting date that is sooner/later than July 1, 2011, etc. Please make an effort to word your footnotes in a manner consistent with notes appearing in the published report, so that ARL can interpret your footnotes correctly.

Please return the completed questionnaire to the
ARL Statistics and Assessment Program by **October 1, 2011.**

For assistance, contact Martha Kyrillidou (martha@arl.org), Shaneka Morris (shaneka@arl.org), Gary Roebuck (gary@arl.org) or David Green (david@arl.org).
Tel: 202-296-2296 or Fax: 202-872-0884.
http://www.arl.org/stats/annualsurveys/salary/

ARL Annual Salary Survey 2011-12
University Library Questionnaire

Note: This is a copy of the form that you will submit electronically at:
http://www.formstack.com/forms/?1093982-c6BynijupA

Part I: Summary Data

Reporting Institution _____ Date Returned to ARL _____

Report Prepared by (name) _____

Title _____

Email address _____ Phone number _____

Contact person (if different) _____

Title _____

Email address Phone number _____

(**Note:**   *ARL will calculate the **2011-12 median and average** professional salaries for your library from the individual data you supply in Part II (Excel form) of this questionnaire.*)

1.	**Beginning Professional Salary**	**Main**	**Law**	**Health**
	Beginning professional salary for 2011-12	_____	_____	_____

(**Note:**   *The Information shown below must be completed for all three branches (i.e. Main, Law and Health Science Libraries) in Part1of the online form.*)

2.   **Rank Structure**

Indicate the number of levels in your institution's rank structure for professional librarians.   **You should report here the maximum number of rank levels, reported in Part II for individual data, under the Rank column.**

_____ 1 level (i.e., no differentiated levels)

_____ 2 levels

_____ 3 levels

_____ 4 levels

_____ 5 levels

_____ more than 5 levels (please specify the number of levels: _____)

3. FOOTNOTES

3a. Please list which libraries are included in the data submitted for the "general" libraries. These can be main campus libraries or branch campus libraries.

3b. Please list which libraries are NOT included in the data submitted for the "general" libraries. These can be main campus libraries or branch campus libraries.

Please indicate any other explanatory information in footnotes. These additional footnotes, if necessary, should be placed in the space below or on attached pages.

Please submit the completed questionnaire to the web form at:
http://www.formstack.com/forms/?1093982-c6BynijupA
by **October 1, 2011.**

For assistance, contact Martha Kyrillidou (martha@arl.org), Shaneka Morris (shaneka@arl.org),
Gary Roebuck (gary@arl.org) or David Green (david@arl.org).
Tel: 202-296-2296 or Fax: 202-872-0884

ARL Annual Salary Survey 2011-2012
University Library Questionnaire

Part II: Individual Data

Note: This is a copy of the Excel form that you will submit electronically at:
http://www.formstack.com/forms/?1093982-c6BynijupA

Confidential									Ethnicity	Race:	Race:	Race:	Race:	Race:	Race:
Detach or delete before submitting to ARL.															
Name/ID	Line	Salary	Job	Sex	OEO cat	Yrs Exp	Rank	Percent	Hispanic or Latino	NatAm	Asian	Black	HawPI	White
	1													
	2													
	3													
	4													
	5													
	6													
	7													
	8													
	9													
	10													
	11													
	12													
	13													
	14													
	15													
	16													
	17													
	18													
	19													
	20													
	21													
	22													
	23													
	24													
	25													

Duplicate this sheet if you need additional lines. Please upload the completed Excel file at the web form at:
http://www.formstack.com/forms/?1093982-c6BynijupA

For assistance, contact Martha Kyrillidou (martha@arl.org), Shaneka Morris (shaneka@arl.org),
Gary Roebuck (gary@arl.org) or David Green (david@arl.org).
Tel: 202-296-2296 or Fax: 202-872-0884

NONUNIVERSITY LIBRARY QUESTIONNAIRE AND INSTRUCTIONS

ASSOCIATION OF RESEARCH LIBRARIES

ARL ANNUAL SALARY SURVEY 2011-12
Nonuniversity Library Questionnaire
GENERAL AND DATA INPUT (EXCEL) INSTRUCTIONS

http://www.arl.org/stats/annualsurveys/salary/

1. This survey is concerned with the salaries of professional positions only.   Since the criteria for determining professional status vary among libraries, there is no attempt to define the term "professional."   Each library should report the salaries of those staff members it considers professionals, irrespective of membership in a collective bargaining unit, and including, when appropriate, staff who are not librarians in the strict sense of the term, such as systems analysts, budget officers, etc.

2. **Obtain the Word file.** These instructions assume that you have Microsoft Word available for use.   If not, or if you have trouble opening the files in Word, please call the ARL Statistics and Assessment Program at (202) 296-2296 or email stats@arl.org.

3. The template Word file is available at: http://www.arl.org/stats/annualsurveys/salary/salform11.shtml. This is a generic, blank form that can hold your data.   The file's name is "sal11_nuform.doc"; open the file and save it to your own computer by choosing "Save As" under the File menu.   When saving the file, utilize ARL as the prefix, use 11 to designate the year (2011-12), and change the "xxxx" in its name to your ARL institution code number, e.g., "ARL119975.doc."

4. Salaries should be reported for all filled positions.   Vacant positions should be excluded from your report.

5. Report 2011-12 salaries *as they exist on July 1, 2011*.   If the library normally increases salaries at a date after July 1, and the salary as of that later date is known or can be estimated (within $100 or so) by the time the questionnaire is due to be returned, please use the higher salary and footnote the effective date and/or whether the reported figures are known or estimated.   Please do not hold up the reporting process for later salary adjustments.

6. The Median Salary is the salary that has an equal number of salaries above it and below it. In those libraries with an even number of positions, the median salary is the average of the two salaries that have an equal number of salaries above and below them.

7. The Beginning Professional Salary is the salary that would be paid to a professional without experience, not necessarily the lowest professional salary paid.   In reporting the beginning salary, please use a figure that is actually used or likely to be used for entry-level librarians hired by your library.

8. Salaries should be reported for both full-time and part-time professional positions.   However, salaries for part-time positions should be converted to their full-time equivalents before reporting; do not report the actual part-time salary paid.

9. Salaries should normally be reported on a 12-month basis.   If an appointment is for 9 or 10 months at the option of the employee, the actual salary paid should be increased to its 12-month equivalent.   However, if appointments of less than 12 months are required by the employer, report the actual salary paid.

10. The salaries for all professional positions should be included, regardless of whether the salaries come from

ASSOCIATION OF RESEARCH LIBRARIES

regular library budget funds or from special funds such as research grants.

11. The salary figures should be straight gross salary figures. Do not include fringe benefits.

12. Explanatory footnotes to the reported figures may be provided when necessary. Footnotes will be included in the published survey.

13. Provide the name of the reporting library and the name of the person who prepares the report.

14. On the second page of the questionnaire (Part II) indicate the number of filled professional positions in each salary range for fiscal years 2010-11 and 2011-12.

15. **Use the newly available Web form for your data submission:**
Non University Libraries: http://www.formstack.com/forms/?1093976-c6BynijupA. Upload your Survey Form through the same interface. NOTE: You must complete the entire submission in a single session. The Web interface does **NOT** allow you to return and edit your information once it is submitted.

Note: ARL is using the online services of FormStack to collect the data. As part of its privacy policy, FormStack pledges not to sell any collected information to third parties. For the complete FormStack privacy policy, visit http://www.formstack.com/privacy.html. ARL also accepts Part I and Part II of the salary survey by e-mail attachment from those users who may be uncomfortable submitting the files in FormStack.

Please Submit the Web form by October 1, 2011.

For assistance, contact Martha Kyrillidou (martha@arl.org), Shaneka Morris (shaneka@arl.org),
Gary Roebuck (gary@arl.org) or David Green (david@arl.org).
Tel: 202-296-2296 or Fax: 202-872-0884

ARL Annual Salary Survey 2011-12
Nonuniversity Library Questionnaire

Note: This is a copy of the form that you will submit electronically at:
http://www.formstack.com/forms/?1093976-c6BynijupA

Part I: Summary Data

Reporting Institution _____ Date Returned to ARL_____

Report Prepared by (name) _____

Title _____

Email address _____ Phone number_____

Contact person (if different) _____

Title _____

Email address _____ Phone number_____

1. Complete the table on the back of this sheet by indicating the number of filled or temporarily vacant professional positions in each salary range for fiscal years 2010-11 and 2011-12.

2. Median professional salary for fiscal year 2011-12: _____

3. Beginning professional salary for 2011-12: _____

4. Footnotes (please compare with footnotes from surveys of previous years)

   a. Law Library salaries are included.

      _____ Yes   _____ No   _____ We do not have a Law Library.

   b. Medical Library salaries are included.

      _____ Yes   _____ No   _____ We do not have a Medical Library.

   c. Branch libraries not included (please attach an additional sheet if necessary):

      _____

      _____

5. Other comments (please attach an additional sheet if necessary):

   _____

   _____

Part II Salaries:

Indicate the number of filled professional positions in each salary range for fiscal years 2010-11 and 2011-12.

Salary Range	Number of Positions	
	2010-11	2011-12
More than 300,000		
250,000 - 299,999		
200,000 - 250,000		
175,000 - 199,999		
150,000 - 174,999		
140,000 - 149,999		
130,000 - 139,999		
120,000 - 129,999		
110,000 - 119,999		
100,000 - 109,999		
95,000 - 99,999		
90,000 - 94,999		
85,000 - 89,999		
80,000 - 84,999		
78,000 - 79,999		
76,000 - 77,999		
74,000 - 75,999		
72,000 - 73,999		
70,000 - 71,999		
68,000 - 69,999		
66,000 - 67,999		
64,000 - 65,999		
62,000 - 63,999		
60,000 - 61,999		
58,000 - 59,999		
56,000 - 57,999		
54,000 - 55,999		
52,000 - 53,999		
50,000 - 51,999		
48,000 - 49,999		
46,000 - 47,999		
44,000 - 45,999		
42,000 - 43,999		
40,000 - 41,999		
38,000 - 39,999		
36,000 - 37,999		
34,000 - 35,999		
less than 34,000		
Total Number of Positions		

Please submit the completed questionnaire to the web form at:
http://www.formstack.com/forms/?1093976-c6BynijupA
by October 1, 2011.

For assistance, contact Martha Kyrillidou (martha@arl.org), Shaneka Morris (shaneka@arl.org), Gary Roebuck (gary@arl.org) or David Green (david@arl.org).
Tel: 202-296-2296 or Fax: 202-872-0884

Footnotes to the ARL Annual Salary Survey, 2011–2012

All data is as of July 1, 2011 unless otherwise noted.

ALBERTA

Library branches included: Augustana Campus Library, HT Coutts Education Library, Rutherford Humanities & Social Sciences Library, Bibliotheque Saint-Jean Library, Winspear Business Reference Library, Cameron Library (including Financial Systems and Analysis, Science and Technology Library, Office of Staff Development and Training , Information Technology Services, Bibliographic Services, Library Personnel and Research and Special Collections Services), and Access Services (including Document Delivery and Interlibrary Loans).

ARIZONA

Library branches included: Main Library, Science-Engineering Library, Fine Arts Library, and The Center for Creative Photography.

ARIZONA STATE

Library branches included: Main Campus and branch campus libraries.

AUBURN

Library branches included: Main, Art & Architecture, and Veterinary Medicine.

BOSTON COLLEGE

Library branches included: O'Neill, Education Resource Center, Bapst Art Library, Burns Library of Rare Books and Manuscripts, Social Work, and Theology and Ministry.

BRIGHAM YOUNG

Library branches included: Main campus library (Harold B. Lee Library).

BRITISH COLUMBIA

Library branches included: Art+Architecture+Planning; Asian Library; David Lam Management Library; Education Library; Irving K. Barber Learning Centre (IKBLC); Koerner Library (Humanities & Social Sciences, Borrower Services); Music Library; Okanagan Library; Rare Books and Special Collections; Robson Square (UBC Library at Robson Square); Science and Engineering; University Archives; and Xwi7xwa Library (First Nations House of Learning). Note: Technical Services and Systems are included in IKBLC and Woodward.

BROWN

Library branches included: John D.Rockefeller Library, John Hay Library, Orwig Music Library, Sciences Library, & John Carter Brown Library.

CALGARY

Library branches included: Taylor Family Digital Library, MacKimmie Library, Gallagher Library of Geology & Geophysics, Business Library, Downtown Campus Library, Health Information Network Knowledge Centres, The Military Museum Library & Archives, and Doucette Library of Teaching Resources.

Our HR position has been centralized by the University so it is no longer funded by the Libraries.

CALIFORNIA, BERKELEY

Library branches included: Doe, Moffitt, Bancroft, Anthropology, Art History/Classics, Astronomy-Mathematics-Statistics, Bioscience & Natural Resources, Business & Economics, Chemistry, C.V. Starr East Asian Library (including Center for Chinese Studies), Earth

Sciences, Education-Psychology, Engineering, Environmental Design, Music, Optometry, Physics, Public Health (including Health Sciences Information Services & Occupational & Environmental Health) & Social Welfare libraries and the Northern Regional Library Facility.

Library branches not included: Affiliated Libraries: Architectural Visual Resources/CED Visual Resource Center, Continuing Education of the Bar, Earthquake Engineering Research Center, Environmental Design Archives, Ethnic Studies, Gianni Foundation of Agricultural Economics, Institute of Governmental Studies, Institute for Research on Labor and Employment, Institute of Transportation Studies, and various departmental libraries: e.g. French, History, Philosophy, Rhetoric, Slavic Languages and Literature.

Rank Structure for Main: Six levels. The University of California [system-wide] Librarian Series Salary Scale adjusted effective 10/1/2011. In accord with the ARL Annual Salary Survey 2011-2012 criteria, all salary data reported corresponds to salary data in existence on July 1, 2011. Beginning Professional Salary effective 10/1/2011.

CALIFORNIA, DAVIS

Library branches included: Peter J. Shields Library (Davis Campus), Physical Sciences & Engineering Library (Davis Campus), Agricultural & Resource Economics Library (Davis Campus).

Librarians who are department heads as reported on this report received administrative stipends since July 1, 1999, but these stipends were not included until the report of ARL 2009-2010. We are including these stipends in department head's salaries and will continue this method of reporting going forward.

CALIFORNIA, IRVINE

Library branches included: Main

Library branches not included: We currently have no professional librarian positions employed at our Medical library therefore, the salaries of those employees are not included in the report.

CALIFORNIA, LOS ANGELES

Library branches included: Charles E. Young Research Library, Powell Library, Arts Library, and Clark Library.

CALIFORNIA, RIVERSIDE

Library branches included: Rivera Library (serving the College of Humanities, Arts and Social Sciences, School of Education, and the School of Business Administration), and Orbach Science Library (serving the College of Natural & Agricultural Sciences, the College of Engineering, and Biomedical Sciences).

Library branches not included: Media and Music Libraries (there are no librarian employees in these facilities).

CALIFORNIA, SAN DIEGO

Library branches included: Social Sciences & Humanities Library, Scripps Institution of Oceanography, Arts Library, Special Collections Library, and Science & Engineering Library.

Librarians who are department heads have received administrative stipends since July 1, 1999. The monthly stipend amount is determined by the number of FTE's in the department.

CALIFORNIA, SANTA BARBARA

Library branches included: Main, Arts.

There are eight levels in the University of California, Santa Barbara's rank structure.

CASE WESTERN RESERVE

Library branches included: Kelvin Smith Library - Main Library, Kulas Music Library, Harris Library, and Mandel School of Applied Social Sciences.

CHICAGO

Library branches included: We include the Law library and the science libraries (including Health) in "Main," we do not break out any data.

CINCINNATI

Library branches included: Survey statistics include all University of Cincinnati Libraries including the Main library, eight college and departmental libraries (Archives and Rare Books, Chemistry-Biology, Classics, Design, Architecture, Art and Planning, Education, Criminal Justice and Human Services, Engineering and Applied Science, Geology-Mathematics-Physicis, and Music), and two regional campus libraries (Clermont College and Raymond Walter College).

COLORADO

Library branches included: Norlin Library (Main); Business Library; Earth Science Library; Engineering, Math, & Physics Library; and Music Library.

Engineering and Math/Physics Libraries were combined in June 2011.

The Beginning Professional Salary (BPS) reported for the Law Library is for librarians with an MLS alone. The beginning salary for librarians with an MLS and JD is $54,000.

COLORADO STATE

Last July (2010), we integrated our department of Academic Computing and Networking Services into CSU Libraries as its own, distinct department inside Libraries. We did this for both practical and strategic reasons: because more and more of that department›s activities were directly supporting CSU Libraries, and also because we are expanding the scope of CSU libraries into more emphasis on digital information. This has been accomplished with the support of the Provost who accepted the strategic plan where this was proposed, and is now codified in our central administrative systems.

COLUMBIA

Library branches included: All Libraries.

CONNECTICUT

Library branches included: University of Connecticut Greater Hartford Campus, Harleigh B Trecker Library, University of Connecticut at Avery Point Library, University of Connecticut at Stamford, Jeremy Richard Library, University at Connecticut at Torrington Library, University of Connecticut at Waterbury Library, University of Connecticut at Storrs, Music & Dramatic Arts Library, University of Connecticut at Storrs, Pharmacy Library, University of Connecticut at Storrs, and Art & Design Library.

CORNELL

Library branches included: Africana, Engineering/Physical Sciences, Fine Arts Library, Geneva Experiment Station, Hotel Administration, Management, Mann Library, Math, Music, ILR, Olin/Krock/Uris, and Veterinary Medicine.

DARTMOUTH

Library branches included: Baker-Berry Library, Feldberg Business & Engineering Library, Sherman Arts Library, Paddock Music Library, Storage Library, Rauner Special Collections Library, and Kresge Physical Sciences Library.

DUKE

Library branches included: Perkins/Bostock Libraries; Rare Book, Manuscript and Special Collections Library; Lilly Library, Music Library, and Divinity School Library.

Library branches not included: Business School/Ford.

EMORY

Library branches included: Main, Theology, Oxford College.

FLORIDA

Library branches included: Included in Main Library - Education, Music, Journalism, Architecture & Fine Arts, Science, Government Documents, Maps, Special and Area Studies Collections, and Humanities and Social Sciences.

There are six ranks at the University of Florida Libraries.

FLORIDA STATE

Library branches included: Strozier Library (Main), Dirac Science Library, and Engineering Library.

Library branches not included: Music; Career Center; Panama City, Panama; Panama City, FL; Ringling; and Goldstein: School of Library and Information Studies.

Rank Structure for the Main library has six levels. The Medical Library reported a beginning salary range: $40K -$42K. Public Services Librarians in Undergraduate Services and Scholars Commons function as a management team. These librarians do perform management and supervisory duties.

GEORGE WASHINGTON

Library branches included: Main.

GEORGETOWN

Libraries included: Bio Ethics Library.

There are two levels in the Law Library's rank structure.

GEORGIA

Library branches included: Main Library, Science Library, Map Library, Student Learning Center Library, Curriculum Learning Center Library, and several reading rooms and experiment station libraries located around the State of Georgia. [Main Library]

Nine levels used for rank structure [Law Library].

GEORGIA TECH

Library branches included: Main Library, and Architecture Branch Library.

GUELPH

Library branches included: Main Campus Libraries: McLaughlin Library and Branch Campus Libraries (which includes the Ridgetown Campus Library).

All salary values listed in Canadian Dollars ($CAD). Individual rank data have been included for professional librarians only: Library Director assigned rank = 0, Assistant Librarian assigned rank = 1, Associate Librarian assigned rank = 2, Librarian assigned rank = 3, Non-librarian professionals assigned rank = 9. Seven Non-librarian professional positions are co-funded by the Library budget, each at 0.52 FTE.

HARVARD

For our «Main» Library submission we used a rank of 1–8 as we have in previous years.

HAWAII

There are four ranks in the University of Hawaii's rank structure: Ranks II–V.

Editor›s Note: Average Years of Experience was reported incorrectly in the 2010-2011 publication for the Law Library. The corrected figure for 2010-2011 is 16.6.

HOUSTON

Library branches included: MD Anderson Library, Architecture & Art Library, Music Library, and Weston A. Pettey Optometry Library.

HOWARD

Library branches included: Founders Library, Undergraduate Library, Architecture Library, Business Library, Divinity Library, and Social Work Library.

Library branches not included: Moorland Spingarn Research Center (autonomous special collection).

Salary data for professional staff on board on July 2011.

ILLINOIS, CHICAGO

Library branches included: The Richard J. Daley Library ("Main" Library).

Rank delineation: Academic Professional – 9, Professor – 4, Associate Professor – 3, Assistant Professor – 2, Instructor – 1, University Librarian/AUL – 0. Tenure and Clinical Track Professors have been combined into one category: "Professor." Tenure and Clinical Track Associate Professors have been combined into one category: "Associate Professor." Tenure and Clinical Track Assistant Professors have been combined into one category: "Assistant Professor."

INDIANA

Library branches included: Main campus libraries.

Library branches not included: Dentistry Library; IUPUI University Library; Herron School of Art Library; Columbus Library; and Science and Engineering Library; and other campuses libraries at IU-East, IU-Kokomo, IU-Northwest, IU-Southeast, IU-South Bend, and IPFW-Fort Wayne.

IOWA

Library branches included: Main & six branches - one campus.

IOWA STATE

Library branches included: 1) Parks Library = Main Library and 2) Veterinary Medical Library = branch library

JOHNS HOPKINS

Library branches included: Sheridan Libraries, Freidheim Library, and SAIS Library.

KANSAS

Library branches included: Includes Lawrence Main campus and Regents Center Library, and Edwards Campus (Overland Park, KS).

KENT STATE

Library branches included: Kent campus - Main, architecture, chemistry/physics, fashion, map, and performing arts libraries.

Library branches not included: Kent State University regional campus libraries.

Kent State University regional campus libraries' information was not included this year, although it has been included in the past. This decision was made because these libraries operate independently: they do not report through Kent campus library; they have separate hiring, tenure/promotion decisions; their budgets are independent of Kent campus.

KENTUCKY
Library branches included: Young Library (Main), Special Collections, Design, Fine Arts, Science, Engineering, Agricultural Information Center, Morris Library (Equine), and Transportation.

The Beginning Professional Salary (BPS) reported for the Law Library is for librarians with an MLS alone. The beginning salary for librarians with an MLS and JD is $52,000.

LAVAL
Library branches included: Main library

LOUISIANA STATE
Library branches included: General libraries include Middleton and Hill Memorial libraries on the main LSU campus.

Beginning salaries for Law librarians are dependent on credentials required.

LOUISVILLE
Library branches included: Art Library, Ekstrom Library (Main), Music Library, and University Archives & Records Center.

In the past, the numbers in the Rank field were assigned based on position in the organization. Beginning this year, the data in this field have been assigned based on academic rank. Also, in the past, the directors of the Health Sciences and the Law Libraries have been assigned a 0 in the rank field, but beginning this year, only the Dean of Libraries has been assigned a 0. The other two library directors have been assigned a rank based on their academic rank.

MCGILL
Library branches included: Education, Islamic Studies, Marvin Duchow Music Library; Birks Reading Room, Walter Hitschfeld Geographic Information Centre; Howard Ross Library of Management; Schulich Library of Science & Engineering; Humanities & Social Sciences Library, and Macdonald Campus (Agricultural & Environmental Sciences).

MCMASTER
Library branches included: Mills Library, Innis Library, and Thode Library.

MANITOBA
Library branches included: William R. Newman Library (Agriculture); Architecture/Fine Arts Library; Elizabeth Dafoe Library; Fr. Harold Drake Library; St. John's College Library; Donald W. Craik Engineering Library; Albert D. Cohen Management Library; Eckhardt-Gramatte Music Library; Sciences and Technology Library; Bill Larson Library; Carolyn Sifton-Helene Fuld Library; Concordia Hospital Library; J.W. Crane Memorial Library; Misercordia Health Centre Library; Seven Oaks General Hospital Library; and Victoria General Hospital Library.

MASSACHUSETTS
Library branches included: DuBois Library (Main library), Image Collection Library, and Science and Engineering Library.

MIT
The rank 7 is currently and frequently unoccupied.

The average salary for those in rank 1 is higher than rank 2. Those in rank 1 are library supervisors, who supervise anywhere from 5-12 people, participate in many of the same committees and activities as professional librarians, but they are not professional librarians. While they occupy the same classification as Librarian 1s within our institutional structure, we have traditionally ranked them for purposes of the survey as the beginning rank since these positions were initially created, many years ago, as promotional opportunities for high level support staff, many of whom were pursuing library degrees. However, some have opted to stay in those positions for their career so their salaries have increased as a result of longevity.

MIAMI

Library branches included: Main library consists of Richter Library, Music, Architecture, Marine and Business.

MICHIGAN

Library branches included: Area Programs; Art, Architecture and Engineering; Asia; Askwith Media; Biological Station; Buhr Remote Shelving Facility; Clark Library for Maps, Government Information and Spatial and Numeric Data Services; Fine Arts; Hatcher Graduate; Museums; Music; Papyrology; Shapiro Science; Shapiro Undergraduate; Special Collections; and Sumner and Laura Foster (Economics).

Library branches not included: Bentley Historical (U-M archives and State of Michigan history); William L. Clements (American history); Gerald R. Ford Presidential; Kresge Business Administration; Mardigian (Dearborn campus); Spectrum/Intergroup Relations; Thompson (Flint campus); UM Transportation Research Institute; and Weill Hall Reading Room (Margaret Dow Towsley Reading Room, Gerald R. Ford School of Public Policy).

Data for the Main and Health Science Libraries are as of September 1, 2011.

Beginning professional salary is $49,000 for librarians without a J.D. degree. Beginning salary with a J.D. degree is $62,000.

MICHIGAN STATE

Library branches included: Main library and 4 branch library locations.

MISSOURI

Library branches included: Main Library, Engineering Library, Journalism Library, Vet Med Library and University Archives.

MONTREAL

Library branches included: Environmental Development (www.bib.umontreal.ca/AM), Botany (www.bib.umontreal.ca/BV), Chemistry (www.bib.umontreal.ca/CH), Educational Resources Library (www.bib.umontreal.ca/DI), Education-Communication-Psychology-Psychoeducation-Biology Library (www.bib.umontreal.ca/ED), Geography (www.bib.umontreal.ca/GP), Kinesiology (www.bib.umontreal.ca/SA), Humanities and Social Sciences (www.bib.umontreal.ca/SS), Rare books and Special Collections (www.bib.umontreal.ca/GP), Mathematics and Computer Sciences (www.bib.umontreal.ca/MI), Veterinary (www.bib.umontreal.ca/SA), Music (www.bib.umontreal.ca/MU), Optometry (www.bib.umontreal.ca/SA), Physics (www.bib.umontreal.ca/PY), École Polytechnique Library (Affiliated School) (www.polymtl.ca), and HEC Montreal Library (Affiliated School)(www.hec.ca).

Library branches not included: Paramedics (www.bib.umontreal.ca/SA).

An error occurred last year for Main beginning professional salary: It should have been inscribed $44,128 instead of $45,915.

NEW MEXICO

Library branches included: Centennial Science & Engineering Library, Fine Arts & Design Library, Parish Memorial Library, and Zimmerman Library.

NEW YORK UNIVERSITY

Library branches included: Elmer Holmes Bobst Library, Courant Institute of Mathematical Sciences, Jack Brause Library, Institute of Fine Arts Library, and Institute for Study of the Ancient World.

Library branches not included: Bern Dibner Library at Polytechnic Institute of NYU, and Abu-Dhabi Library.

The three ranks for faculty positions are as follows: 1) Library Associate, 2) Assistant Curator, 3) Associate Curator.

NORTH CAROLINA STATE

Library branches included: (Main) D.H. Hill Library, Design Library, Natural Resources Library, Textiles Library, and Veterinary Medicine Library.

NORTHWESTERN

Library branches included: University Library organization, which includes all Northwestern University Libraries.

Northwestern implemented a system of ranks for librarian faculty September 1, 2011. The ranks (librarian, senior librarian, assistant/ associate director, and director) correspond with job duties, not professional attainment by individual librarians. [Main Library]

Salary data is for FY12, beginning September 1, 2011. This is the first year for which Northwestern University assigns ranks for librarians, based on job descriptions. [Law Library]

These data are for FY 2011-2012, which for us began on September 1, 2011. [Health Sciences Library]

NOTRE DAME

Library branches included: The Hesburgh Libraries of Notre Dame include all libraries located within the primary campus of the University.

Library branches not included: University Archives has not been included.

OHIO UNIVERSITY

Library branches included: Main campus, Learning Resource Center (College of Medicine) and Branch campuses: Lancaster, Southern, Chillicothe, and Eastern and Zanesville.

OHIO STATE

Library branches included: Main and Lima campus.

Library branches not included: Ohio Agricultural Research & Development Center, Agriculture Technical Inst.(ATI), Mansfield Campus, Marion Campus, and Newark Campus.

The rank structure has changed this year to better reflect the academic structure at OSU: 0 = director, 1 = instructor/visiting assistant professor, 2 = assistant professor, 3 = associate professor, 4 = professor.

OKLAHOMA

Library branches included: Branch Libraries: Architecture, Engineering, Fine Arts, Geology, and Physics/Astronomy.

OKLAHOMA STATE

Library branches included: OSU-Stillwater including Veterinary Medicine, Curriculum Materials, and Architecture libraries; OSU-Oklahoma City, OSU-Okmulgee (i.e., OSU-Tech), and OSU-Tulsa.

OREGON
Library branches included: Knight Library, Science Libraries, Architecture & Allied Arts Library, and Portland Library & Learning Commons.

OTTAWA
Library branches included: Main Library.

Library branches not included: Satellite Management Library.

As of April 30, 2011, the Librarian' Collective Agreement has expired and negotiations are still ongoing.

PENNSYLVANIA
Library branches included: University Library, Lippinoctt Business Library, Math/Physics/Physical Sciences, Fine Arts, Veterinary, Museum, Center For Advanced Judaic Studies, Rarebook And Manuscript, and Music.

Library branches not included: Annenberg Communications.

PENNSYLVANIA STATE
Library branches included: University Park (main campus), Abington, Altoona, Beaver, Berks, Brandywine, DuBois, Erie, Fayette, Great Valley, Greater Allegheny, Harrisburg, Hazleton, Lehigh Valley, Mont Alto, New Kensington, Shenango, Schuylkill, Wilkes-Barre, Worthington Scranton, and York.

PITTSBURGH
Library branches included: University Library System and library directors at regional libraries - Titusville, Johnstown, Bradford, Greensburg.

PRINCETON
Library branches included: Architecture Library, East Asian Library and the Gest Collection, Engineering Library, Firestone Library, Forrestal Annex (Annex A), Furth Plasma Physics Library, Humanities Resource Center (Video Librariy), Lewis Library, Marquand Library of Art and Archaeology, Mendel Music Library, Mudd Manuscript Library, ReCAP (Research Collections and Preservation Consortium), and the Stokes Library (Public and International Affairs and Population Research).

PURDUE
Library branches included: Includes the library system on the West Lafayette campus, consisting of 11 subject libraries, an undergraduate library and the Virginia Kelly Karnes Archives and Special Collections Research Center.

Library branches not included: Excludes libraries at the regional campuses: Purdue North Central (Westville), Purdue Calumet (Hammond), Indiana University-Purdue University Fort Wayne, and Indiana University-Purdue University Indianapolis.

QUEEN'S
Library branches included: General (Main) libraries includes: Stauffer (Humanities & Social Sciences), Douglas (Engineering/Science), Jordan (Special Collections/Music), and Education.

ROCHESTER
Library branches included: Includes River Campus Libraries & Sibley Music Library.

RUTGERS
Editor's note: Library branches included was incorrectly reported in the 2010-2011 publication. The following lists represent the corrected list of libraries included and not included in the submission for Rutgers for the 2010-2011 and the 2011-2012 Salary Surveys.

Library branches included: Research and Instructional Services (which includes the Alexander Library, Mabel Smith Douglass Library, Kilmer Library, and the Library of Science and Medicine and Branches); John Cotton Dana Library; Paul Robeson Library; and Technical and Automated Services.

Library branches not included: School for Management and Labor Relations, and the Center for Alcohol Studies.

SASKATCHEWAN

Library branches included: Murray Library; Education & Music Library; Natural Sciences Library; Veterinary Medicine Library; Engineering Library; and University Archives.

SOUTH CAROLINA

Library branches included: Thomas Cooper Library, Business Library, Math Library, Music Library, Hollings Special Collections Library, Moving Image Research Collections, and South Caroliniana Library.

SOUTHERN CALIFORNIA

Library branches included: Accounting, Architecture and Fine Arts, Business, Cinematic Arts, Doheny Memorial Library, East Asian Library, Education and Social Work Libraries, Gerontology, Grand Library, Leavey Library, Music Library, Hoose Philosophy Library, Science & Engineering Library, Special Collections, and Von KleinSmid Library (VKC).

SUNY-ALBANY

Library branches included: University Library – Main, Dewey Library – branch, Science Library – branch.

SUNY-BUFFALO

Library branches included: Includes the Arts & Sciences Library, Music Library, and Special Collections (Archives, Poetry and Rare Books).

Excludes temporary hires, classified staff and staff at the SL-2 salary level.

SUNY-STONY BROOK

Library branches included: The Main campus library and four branch libraries.

SYRACUSE

Library branches included: Main campus library, Science & Technology Library, and Geology & Math Libraries.

TEMPLE

Library branches included: General or main library includes Paley Library, Ambler Library, Science & Engineering Library, and the Charles L. Blockson Afro-American Collection.

For Main library the minimum beginning salary of $44,044 is based on an 11 month contract. the minimum beginning salary for a 10 month contract is $40,150 should the librarian elect that contract term at time of hire.

TENNESSEE

Library branches included: Includes Hodges Main Library, Pendergrass Agriculture and Veterinary Medicine Library, and Devine Music Library.

The Memphis Health Sciences Library has a five-level rank structure and the Knoxville Hospital Preston Medical Library has a three-level rank structure. [Main Library, Knoxville Health Sciences Library, Memphis Health Sciences Library]. Health Sciences Library data includes the Knoxville Health Sciences Library and the Memphis Health Sciences Library, reported separately.

TEXAS

Library branches included: UT Libraries, Harry Ransom Center, and Dolph Briscoe Center for American History.

Data is for September 1, 2011.

TEXAS A&M

Library branches included: Cushing Memorial Library, Library Annex, Medical Sciences Library, Sterling C. Evans Library, and West Campus Library.

TEXAS TECH

Library branches included: University Library, Architecture Library, and Vietnam Archives.

Salaries are as of 9/1/11. The Health Sciences Center Libraries report a five-level structure of rank.

VANDERBILT

Library branches included: The data submitted includes the Central Library, Divinity Library, Peabody Library, Management Library, Music Library, Science and Engineering Library, Special Collections and University Archives, centralized Technical Services, Library Administration and the Television News Archive.

VIRGINIA

Library branches included: Darden Graduate Business, Alderman (Main), Astronomy, Biology/Psychology, Chemistry, Clemons Undergraduate, Education, Fiske Kimball Fine Arts, Math, Music, Physics, Brown Science & Engineering, and Small Special Collections.

Library branches not included: University of Virginia's College at Wise.

VIRGINIA TECH

Library branches included: Newman Library, Vet Med Library, Art and Architecture Library.

WASHINGTON

Library branches included: Includes libraries on the Seattle, Bothell, and Tacoma campuses of the University of Washington.

WASHINGTON STATE

Library branches included: WSU Pullman, WSU Spokane, WSU Vancouver, WSU Tri-Cities, and WSU Energy Library.

WASHINGTON U.-ST. LOUIS

Library branches included: Main Library includes: Central Library, Art & Architecture Library, Business Library, Chemistry Library, East Asian Library, Earth and Planetary Sciences Library, Music Library, Physics Library, Social Work Library, and West Campus Library.

WATERLOO

Library branches included: Dana Porter Library, Davis Centre Library, University Map Library, Musagetes, and Architecture Library.

We have a six-level rank structure.

WAYNE STATE

Library branches included: The "general libraries" include the Purdy/Kresge Library, Science and Engineering Library, and Undergraduate Library.

Library branches not included: The Reuther Archives of Labor and Urban Affairs.

The Wayne State University Libraries have reported fewer positions this year for two reasons. Twelve positions that we had previously reported have been removed from these figures; though those positions are part of our wider University Library System organization, we no longer identify them as part of the University Libraries proper. Three positions were lost due to a university wide reduction in labor force.

WESTERN ONTARIO

Library branches included: C.B. "Bud" Johnston Library (Business Library), Education Library, Music Library, The D.B.Weldon Library (Arts & Humanities, Social Sciences, Journalism, Library Sciences), Allyn and Betty Taylor Library (Medicine, Nursing, Dental, Health Sciences, Engineering), Map and Data Centre, Archives, and Affiliated University College.

Libraries are not included: Brescia University College Library, Huron University College Library, King's University College Library, and St. Peter's Seminary College Library.

WISCONSIN

Library branches included: Archives, College, Steenbock Agricultural and Life Science, Art, Biology, Business, Chemistry, Geography, Geology, Math, Merit (Education), Music, Physics, Social Work, Special collections, Social Science Reading Room, Wendt Engineering, WiLS (Wisconsin Library Services).

Rank Structure:
1   Assoc Academic Lib or AIPC
2   Academic Lib/IPC
3   Sr Acad Lib/SIPC
4   Distinguished Librarian
5   Asst/Assoc Dir
6   Director
7   Deputy Director
8   NA
9   Employees outside the ranking system [Main Library], such as contractual positions (i.e. Japanese Bib) [Law and Health Science Library]
0   Director [Main Library]

YALE

Library branches included: Haas Arts Library, Bass Library, Beinecke Rare Book & Manuscript Library, Classics Library, Divinity School Library, Engineering & Applied Science Library, Government Documents & Information Center, Lewis Walpole Library [site], Mudd Library, Music Library, Kline Science Library, Social Science Library, and Sterling Memorial Library.

Data are as of 1/25/2012. [Law Library]

BOSTON PUBLIC LIBRARY

All branches included.

LIBRARY OF CONGRESS

Law Library salaries are included in the 2011-2012 data. Editor's note: Law Library salaries were also included in the 2010-2011 data, but this footnote was omitted in error.

Salaries include Professional and Administrative positions.

NATIONAL AGRICULTURAL LIBRARY

Editor's note: For the 2010-2011 and 2011-2012 Salary Surveys, all salaries are those held with benefits. The 2010-2011 footnote was omitted in error.

NATIONAL ARCHIVES

Survey includes ALL 44 NARA locations nation-wide: www.archives.gov/locations. "Professional" determined by Office of Personnel Management definition: www.opm.gov/qualifications/standards/group-stds/gs-prof.asp

NEW YORK PUBLIC LIBRARY

We did not include our Branch Libraries, nor did we include any positions in Administration (Budget, Finance, etc). We included Professionals and 1st level managers only.

NEW YORK STATE LIBRARY

Editor's note: For the 2010-2011 and 2011-2012 Salary Surveys, Law and Medical Library salaries are included in the data. The 2010-2011 footnote was omitted in error.

ARL Member Libraries as of January 1, 2012

The Association of Research Libraries (ARL) represents the interests of 126 libraries that serve major North American research institutions. ARL operates as a forum for the exchange of ideas and as an agent for collective action to influence the forces affecting the ability of these libraries to meet the future needs of scholarship. The ARL Statistics and Assessment program is organized around identifying, collecting, analyzing, and distributing quantifiable information describing the characteristics of research libraries. The program offers publications and special member services, and collaborates with other national and international library statistics programs.

Institution	Category	Full Name of Institution	Location
Alabama	S	University of Alabama	Tuscaloosa, Alabama
Alberta	C	University of Alberta	Edmonton, Alberta
Arizona	S	University of Arizona	Tucson, Arizona
Arizona State	S	Arizona State University	Tempe, Arizona
Auburn	S	Auburn University	Auburn, Alabama
Boston	P	Boston University	Boston, Massachusetts
Boston College	P	Boston College	Boston, Massachusetts
Brigham Young	P	Brigham Young University	Provo, Utah
British Columbia	C	University of British Columbia	Vancouver, British Columbia
Brown	P	Brown University	Providence, Rhode Island
Berkeley, California	S	University of California, Berkeley	California, Berkeley
Calgary	C	University of Calgary	Calgary, Alberta
California, Davis	S	University of California, Davis	Davis, California
California, Irvine	S	University of California, Irvine	Irvine, California
California, Los Angeles	S	University of California, Los Angeles	Los Angeles, California
California, Riverside	S	University of California, Riverside	Riverside, California
California, San Diego	S	University of California, San Diego	La Jolla, California
California, Santa Barbara	S	University of California, Santa Barbara	Santa Barbara, California
Case Western Reserve	P	Case Western Reserve University	Cleveland, Ohio
Chicago	P	University of Chicago	Chicago, Illinois
Cincinnati	S	University of Cincinnati	Cincinnati, Ohio
Colorado	S	University of Colorado	Boulder, Colorado
Colorado State	S	Colorado State University	Fort Collins, Colorado
Columbia	P	Columbia University	New York, New York
Connecticut	S	University of Connecticut	Storrs, Connecticut
Cornell	P	Cornell University	Ithaca, New York
Dartmouth	P	Dartmouth College	Hanover, New Hampshire
Delaware	S	University of Delaware	Newark, Delaware
Duke	P	Duke University	Durham, North Carolina
Emory	P	Emory University	Atlanta, Georgia
Florida	S	University of Florida	Gainesville, Florida
Florida State	S	Florida State University	Tallahassee, Florida
George Washington	P	George Washington University	Washington, DC
Georgetown	P	Georgetown University	Washington, DC

Institution	Category	Full Name of Institution	Location
Georgia	S	University of Georgia	Athens, Georgia
Georgia Tech	S	Georgia Institute of Technology	Atlanta, Georgia
Guelph	C	University of Guelph	Guelph, Ontario
Harvard	P	Harvard University	Cambridge, Massachusetts
Hawaii	S	University of Hawaii	Honolulu, Hawaii
Houston	S	University of Houston	Houston, Texas
Howard	P	Howard University	Washington, DC
Illinois, Chicago	S	University of Illinois at Chicago	Chicago, Illinois
Illinois, Urbana	S	University of Illinois at Urbana	Urbana, Illinois
Indiana	S	Indiana University	Bloomington, Indiana
Iowa	S	University of Iowa	Iowa City, Iowa
Iowa State	S	Iowa State University	Ames, Iowa
Johns Hopkins	P	Johns Hopkins University	Baltimore, Maryland
Kansas	S	University of Kansas	Lawrence, Kansas
Kent State	S	Kent State University	Kent, Ohio
Kentucky	S	University of Kentucky	Lexington, Kentucky
Laval	C	Laval University	Quebec, Quebec
Louisiana State	S	Louisiana State University	Baton Rouge, Louisiana
Louisville	S	University of Louisville	Louisville, Kentucky
McGill	C	McGill University	Montreal, Quebec
McMaster	C	McMaster University	Hamilton, Ontario
Manitoba	C	University of Manitoba	Winnipeg, Manitoba
Maryland	S	University of Maryland	College Park, Maryland
Massachusetts	S	University of Massachusetts	Amherst, Massachusetts
MIT	P	Massachusetts Institute of Technology	Cambridge, Massachusetts
Miami	P	University of Miami	Coral Gables, Florida
Michigan	S	University of Michigan	Ann Arbor, Michigan
Michigan State	S	Michigan State University	East Lansing, Michigan
Minnesota	S	University of Minnesota	Minneapolis, Minnesota
Missouri	S	University of Missouri	Columbia, Missouri
Montreal	C	University of Montreal	Montreal, Quebec
Nebraska	S	University of Nebraska-Lincoln	Lincoln, Nebraska
New Mexico	S	University of New Mexico	Albuquerque, New Mexico
New York	P	New York University	New York, New York
North Carolina	S	University of North Carolina	Chapel Hill, North Carolina
North Carolina State	S	North Carolina State University	Raleigh, North Carolina
Northwestern	P	Northwestern University	Evanston, Illinois
Notre Dame	P	University of Notre Dame	Notre Dame, Indiana
Ohio	S	Ohio University	Athens, Ohio
Ohio State	S	Ohio State University	Columbus, Ohio
Oklahoma	S	University of Oklahoma	Norman, Oklahoma
Oklahoma State	S	Oklahoma State University	Stillwater, Oklahoma

Institution	Category	Full Name of Institution	Location
Oregon	S	University of Oregon	Eugene, Oregon
Ottawa	C	University of Ottawa	Ottawa, Ontario
Pennsylvania	P	University of Pennsylvania	Philadelphia, Pennsylvania
Pennsylvania State	S	Pennsylvania State University	University Park, Pennsylvania
Pittsburgh	S	University of Pittsburgh	Pittsburgh, Pennsylvania
Princeton	P	Princeton University	Princeton, New Jersey
Purdue	S	Purdue University	West Lafayette, Indiana
Queen's	C	Queen's University	Kingston, Ontario
Rice	P	Rice University	Houston, Texas
Rochester	P	University of Rochester	Rochester, New York
Rutgers	S	Rutgers University	New Brunswick, New Jersey
Saskatchewan	C	University of Saskatchewan	Saskatoon, Saskatchewan
South Carolina	S	University of South Carolina	Columbia, South Carolina
Southern California	P	University of Southern California	Los Angeles, California
Southern Illinois	S	Southern Illinois University	Carbondale, Illinois
SUNY-Albany	S	University at Albany, State University of New York	Albany, New York
SUNY-Buffalo	S	University at Buffalo, State University of New York	Buffalo, New York
SUNY-Stony Brook	S	State University of New York at Stony Brook	Stony Brook, New York
Syracuse	P	Syracuse University	Syracuse, New York
Temple	S	Temple University	Philadelphia, Pennsylvania
Tennessee	S	University of Tennessee	Knoxville, Tennessee
Texas	S	University of Texas	Austin, Texas
Texas A&M	S	Texas A&M University	College Station, Texas
Texas Tech	S	Texas Tech University	Lubbock, Texas
Toronto	C	University of Toronto	Toronto, Ontario
Tulane	P	Tulane University	New Orleans, Louisiana
Utah	S	University of Utah	Salt Lake City, Utah
Vanderbilt	P	Vanderbilt University	Nashville, Tennessee
Virginia	S	University of Virginia	Charlottesville, Virginia
Virginia Tech	S	Virginia Polytechnic Institute & State University	Blacksburg, Virginia
Washington	S	University of Washington	Seattle, Washington
Washington State	S	Washington State University	Pullman, Washington
Washington U.-St. Louis	P	Washington University	St. Louis, Missouri
Waterloo	C	University of Waterloo	Waterloo, Ontario
Wayne State	S	Wayne State University	Detroit, Michigan
Western Ontario	C	University of Western Ontario	London, Ontario
Wisconsin	S	University of Wisconsin	Madison, Wisconsin
Yale	P	Yale University	New Haven, Connecticut
York	C	York University	North York, Ontario
Boston Public Library	N	Boston Public Library	Boston, Massachusetts
Canada Inst. SciTech Info.	X	Canada Inst. for Scientific & Technical Information	Ottawa, Ontario

Institution	Category	Full Name of Institution	Location
Center for Research Libs.	N	Center for Research Libraries	Chicago, Illinois
Lib. & Archives Canada	X	Library and Archives Canada	Ottawa, Ontario
Library of Congress	N	Library of Congress	Washington, DC
Natl. Agricultural Lib.	N	National Agricultural Library	Beltsville, Maryland
Natl. Archives & Records	N	National Archives and Records Administration	Washington, DC
Natl. Library of Medicine	N	National Library of Medicine	Bethesda, Maryland
New York Public Library	N	New York Public Library	New York, New York
New York State Library	N	New York State Library	Albany, New York
Smithsonian Institution	N	Smithsonian Institution	Washington, DC

S – US public university
P – US private university
C – Canadian university
N – US nonuniversity
X – Canadian nonuniversity

14419275R00066

Made in the USA
Charleston, SC
10 September 2012